Family Circle | **fast meals cookbook**

Family Circle®

FAST MEALS COOKBOOK

FAMILY CIRCLE LIBRARY OF CREATIVE COOKING

A Practical Guide to creative cooking containing special material from Family Circle Magazine and the Family Circle Illustrated Library of Cooking

ROCKVILLE HOUSE PUBLISHERS
GARDEN CITY, NEW YORK 11530

on the cover:
For a casserole fast meal, try **Brunswick Stew.** It's sure to please every member of the family.

on the title page:
Sicilian Potato Bake is one meal put-together-in-a-hurry that will find satisfied customers.

on the back page:
When short on ideas, bedazzle your company with **Castillian Meatballs in Wine Sauce** (top) and accompany with **Orange Crown Mold.**

Publishing Staff

Editor: MALCOLM E. ROBINSON
Design and Layout: MARGOT L. WOLF
Production Editor: DONALD D. WOLF

For Family Circle

Editorial Director: ARTHUR M. HETTICH
Editor Family Circle Books: MARIE T. WALSH
Assistant Editor: CERI E. HADDA

A QUICK METRIC TABLE FOR COOKS

Liquid Measures

1 liter	4¼ cups (1 quart + ¼ cup or 34 fluid ounces)	1 gallon	3.785 liters
1 demiliter (½ liter)	2⅛ cups (1 pint + ⅛ cups or 17 fluid ounces)	1 quart	0.946 liter
1 deciliter (1/10 liter)	A scant ½ cup or 3.4 fluid ounces	1 pint	0.473 liter
1 centiliter (1/100 liter)	Approximately 2 teaspoons or .34 fluid ounce	1 cup	0.237 liter or 237 milliliters
1 milliliter (1/1000 liter)	Approximately 1/5 teaspoon or .034 fluid ounce	1 tbsp.	Approximately 1.5 centiliters or 15 milliliters

Weights

1 kilogram	2.205 pounds	1 pound	0.454 kilogram or 453.6 grams
500 grams	1.103 pounds or about 17.5 ounces	½ pound	0.226 kilogram or 226.8 grams
100 grams	3.5 ounces	¼ pound	0.113 kilogram or 113.4 grams
10 grams	.35 ounce	1 ounce	28.35 grams
1 gram	0.035 ounce		

Linear Measures

1 meter	1.09 yards or 3.28 feet or 39.37 inches	1 yard	0.914 meter
1 decimeter (1/10 meter)	3.93 inches	1 foot	0.3048 meter or 3.048 decimeters or 30.48 centimeters
1 centimeter (1/100 meter)	0.39 inch	1 inch	2.54 centimeters or 25.4 millimeters
1 millimeter (1/1000 meter)	0.039 inch		

Contents

INTRODUCTION 6

1. COOKING IN MINUTES 7
Appetizers 7
Main Dishes 14
Sandwiches 23
Desserts 33
Menus 50

2. PANTRY SHELF COOKING 65
Soups 65
Vegetables 67
Main Dishes 71
Salads 83
Desserts from Mixes 88

INDEX 95

For an exciting array of hors d'oeuvres, serve **Blini with Sour Cream and Red Caviar, Peruvian Puffs, Boursin-Stuffed Mushrooms, Bite-Size Frankwiches,** and **Guacamole in Cherry Tomatoes.**

Introduction

T ODAY'S PACE is fast, and so are the demands on the kitchen. Whether it's because of the rush for work or for school, or in the evening, the dash for some activity, it seems there just is not time for a meal. Shortchanging your health is almost a way of life. But it doesn't have to be so.

And this is where your **Fast Meals Cookbook** comes into play. In these pages are many recipes and menus, which are whipped up in a hurry. Whatever the circumstance, you will be able to find a recipe that will fit your needs.

Turn to the first section, "Cooking in Minutes," and you'll see appetizers, main dishes, sandwiches, desserts, and even some full-blown menus. All of them are quick-fix recipes, or menus, so that you don't have to spend hours in the kitchen.

The second section, "Pantry Shelf Cooking," is loaded with recipes that take advantage of the convenience foods and mixes that are stocked in the supermarket. Together with blenders and other kitchen short-cut equipment, they enable you to turn out the most fancy-looking dishes in the shortest time.

So enjoy the hectic pace that allows you to do so many of the recreational activities that make up your rich life, but don't forget your stomach—and your life. Use this book properly and you will always have a full stomach—from one of the many recipes and menus in this book that are designed to give you what you need, and fast.

Cooking in Minutes

You've just arrived home and have discovered there's unexpected company. Or your mate calls to say that he or she will bring home a friend. Or the children pop in with several friends, all hungry from the sandlot.

This is the time when your cooking inventiveness comes into play. You must rustle up something fast. In this section are recipes for appetizers, main dishes, sandwiches, and desserts for those-on-call times. And, at the back of the section, a collection of menus that are either make-ahead or quick-fix.

APPETIZERS

Blini with Sour Cream and Red Caviar

Plump little two-bite pancakes lavished with sour cream; you can even make them the night before, refrigerate, then reheat in a low oven until nice and warm

Preparation time: 25 minutes.
Makes 6 dozen.

1 carton (16 ounces) frozen pancake batter, defrosted
1 container (8 ounces) dairy sour cream
1 jar (4¼ ounces) red caviar

1 Heat griddle; grease lightly. Pour approximately 1 teaspoon pancake batter for each blini onto griddle; turn once. Place on cooky sheet. Keep warm between paper toweling in a slow oven while making the miniature pancakes.
2 To serve: Top with a dollop of sour cream and red caviar. Serve warm.

Peruvian Puffs

Savory yet simple filling that may be made hours ahead—use a pastry bag and tube for easy filling

Preparation time: 20 minutes.
Broiling time: 1 minute.
Makes 30 puffs.

½ cup grated Parmesan cheese
½ cup mayonnaise or salad dressing

1½ teaspoons anchovy paste
1 teaspoon minced onion
1 container (3¼ ounces) cocktail-size pastry shells (croutelettes—(about 30)
1 jar (2¾ ounces) tiny cocktail shrimp
Parsley

1 Combine the Parmesan cheese, mayonnaise or salad dressing, anchovy paste and onion in a small bowl.
2 Spoon mixture evenly into cocktail-size pastry shells. Place on jelly-roll pan.
3 Run under broiler until tops are bubbly and beginning to brown, about 1 minute. Garnish with tiny cocktail shrimp and parsley, if you wish. Serve hot.

Boursin-Stuffed Mushrooms

Mellow cheese makes a tasty filling for crispy-fresh mushrooms; these mushrooms will keep their freshness for many hours, so prepare them as early in the day as you wish

Preparation time: 25 minutes.
Makes 3 dozen.

36 small to medium-size fresh mushrooms
3 packages (5 ounces each) Boursin cheese with garlic and fines herbes, softened
Parsley

1 Wipe mushrooms with damp cloth; remove stems, breaking off where they join the cap. (Use the stems for soup.)
2 Spoon cheese into mushrooms, or fill pastry bag and pipe cheese into mushrooms. Garnish with parsley sprig; refrigerate.

Bite-Size Frankwiches

A miniature frank in a bun

Preparation time: 5 minutes.
Baking time: 10 minutes.
Makes 40 hors d'oeuvres.

1 package (11 ounces) baking powder biscuits (10 biscuits)
2 jars (6 ounces each) cocktail-size frankfurters
Spicy brown mustard

(continued)

1 Cut each biscuit into quarters. Place on un-greased cooky sheet, point up.
2 Separate the top of each biscuit quarter slightly and place a cocktail frankfurter in the center. Secure each with a wooden pick.
3 Bake in a hot oven (400°) 10 minutes, or until biscuits are golden brown. Serve hot with a dollop of mustard.

Guacamole in Cherry Tomatoes

Frozen, prepared and mashed avocado makes this appetizer easy

Preparation time: 25 minutes.
Makes about 3 dozen.

1 can (7¾ ounces) frozen avocado, defrosted
2 teaspoons finely chopped green onion
2 teaspoons imitation bacon bits
½ teaspoon Worcestershire sauce
2 pints cherry tomatoes (about 36)
1 jar (5 ounces) cocktail onions

1 Combine avocado, green onion, bacon bits and Worcestershire in a small bowl.
2 Cut thin slice off top of each tomato; scoop out seeds with a melon-ball scoop or small measuring spoon; turn over to drain.
3 Spoon about 1 teaspoon guacamole filling into tomatoes. Garnish each with cocktail onion.

Anchovy Dip for Raw Vegetables

This dip is fast to make and fast to disappear

Preparation time: 10 minutes.
Makes 1½ cups.

1 cup mayonnaise or salad dressing
½ cup chopped watercress
1 can (2 ounces) rolled anchovies with capers
1 clove minced garlic
1 teaspoon grated lemon rind
2 tablespoons lemon juice

Combine all ingredients in a medium-size bowl. Chill. Serve with raw vegetables—radishes, celery and carrot sticks, cherry tomatoes, broccoli flowerets or thinly sliced zucchini.

Oahu Dip-and-Chip Tray

Shape the cheese spread into a "mountain" and frame with raw nibbles and corn dippers or favorite chips.

Makes 16 servings

1½ pounds cream-style cottage cheese (3 cups)
3 packages (8 ounces each) cream cheese, softened
6 ounces blue cheese, crumbled
1 teaspoon seasoned salt
2 teaspoons Worcestershire sauce
Few drops liquid red pepper seasoning
1 cup finely chopped parsley
Pitted ripe olives
1 cherry tomato
4 large carrots, pared and sliced diagonally
2 large cucumbers, scored and sliced
8 stalks celery, sliced
2 large green peppers, quartered, seeded, and cut in bite-size pieces
1 small head of cauliflower, separated in flowerets
Flower-shape corn snacks

1 Combine cottage, cream, and blue cheeses, seasoned salt, Worcestershire sauce, and liquid red pepper seasoning in a large bowl; beat until completely blended; cover. Chill several hours, or until firm enough to handle.
2 Spoon cheese mixture in the center of a large serving tray; pat into a "mountain" shape, then press parsley into cheese to cover the bottom two thirds.
3 Cut olives lengthwise into 8 wedges each; arrange over cheese in a spiral pattern almost to top.
4 Slice cherry tomato into eighths from blossom end almost to stem end; separate cuts slightly to form petals; stand on top of cheese. Arrange carrot, cucumber, and celery slices, green pepper pieces, cauliflowerets, and corn snacks in separate piles around cheese.

Tomato Dip

Canned soup and cream cheese make this dip quick and economical

Makes 2 cups

1 can (10¾-ounces) condensed tomato soup
1 3-ounce package cream cheese, softened
¼ cup chopped ripe olives

Surround **Anchovy Dip for Raw Vegetables** with radishes, celery, cherry tomatoes, carrots or broccoli.

2 tablespoons chopped parsley
⅛ teaspoon pepper

Blend tomato soup and cream cheese in a medium-size bowl until smooth. Stir in remaining ingredients and chill about an hour before serving.

Bean-Onion Dip

This is a dip with a bit of a bite, and a taste of the Southwest

Makes 2 cups

1 can (1 pound) pork-and-beans
1 small onion, peeled and quartered
¼ cup molasses
2 tablespoons prepared mustard

Whirl all ingredients in an electric blender until smooth. (If you do not have a blender, press beans through a sieve; grate the onion instead of quartering, then mix all ingredients together). Serve with crisp crackers.

Sweet-Sour Dip

Keep these ingredients on hand for a dip that's different and quick to make

Makes about 1⅓ cups

4 slices bacon, diced
1 package (8 ounces) cream cheese, softened
¼ cup bottled sweet-sour salad dressing
2 tablespoons milk

1 Sauté bacon until crisp in a small frying pan; remove to paper toweling to drain.
2 Combine cream cheese, salad dressing and milk in a medium-size bowl; beat until smooth. Fold in bacon, chill several hours, then serve with crackers or crisp vegetable sticks.

Guacamole

The dip that has become a "must" at every party

Makes about 2 cups

1 medium-size ripe avocado
½ cup mayonnaise or salad dressing
2 tablespoons lemon juice
1 teaspoon salt
1 teaspoon grated onion
¼ teaspoon liquid red pepper seasoning
1 large tomato, peeled, chopped and drained

1 Halve avocado, peel, pit and mash in a medium-size bowl. Blend in remaining ingredients, cover and chill. (Dip will stay bright green several hours.)
2 When ready to serve, spoon into small bowls and set out plenty of crisp corn sticks.

Clam-Cream Dip

Your zippy seasoning helper? Versatile horseradish dip mix in an envelope

Makes 2 cups

1 cup (8-ounce carton) cream-style cottage cheese
1 package (3 or 4 ounces) cream cheese
1 packet (about 1 tablespoon) horseradish dip mix or 2 teaspoons prepared horseradish
1 teaspoon Worcestershire sauce
1 can (about 10 ½ ounces) minced clams, drained
3 to 4 tablespoons light or table cream
Red caviar

1 Blend cottage cheese, cream cheese, dip mix or horseradish, and Worcestershire sauce in a medium-size bowl; stir in clams. Chill.
2 When ready to serve, beat in cream to thin mixture enough for dipping; spoon into small bowls; top with red caviar. Serve with crisp potato chips, if you wish.

Kauai Crab Spread

Serve this dip, inspired by Hawaii, for a special occasion

Makes about 2½ cups

8 ounces (half a 1-pound package) frozen crab meat, thawed and drained

1 cup dairy sour cream
2 teaspoons curry powder
½ teaspoon onion salt
½ teaspoon garlic powder
¼ cup minced chutney
¼ cup flaked coconut

Mix all ingredients and chill well. Serve as a spread for crackers or melba rounds.

Spanish Tuna Dip

Olives and tuna are a happy combination and sure to be a hit

Makes about 2 cups

½ cup (1 stick) butter or margarine
1 can (about 7 ounces) water-pack tuna, drained and flaked
4 teaspoons lemon juice
¼ cup mayonnaise or salad dressing
2 tablespoons chopped stuffed green olives

1 Cream butter or margarine until soft in a small bowl; beat in tuna, lemon juice, and mayonnaise or salad dressing; fold in olives. Chill.
2 Spoon into small dip bowls. Serve with crisp carrot and celery sticks or crackers.

Garlic Cheese Dip

Three ingredients from your kitchen and two minutes of your time will give you this tasty dip

Makes 2 cups

2 cups (16-ounce carton) dairy sour cream
1 envelope cheese-garlic salad dressing mix
½ teaspoon dried parsley flakes

Combine all ingredients in a small bowl, chill several hours to blend flavors, then serve with crackers or crisp vegetable sticks.

Twin Cheese Molds

Make these ahead and keep on hand for guests who drop in

Makes 12 servings

2 cups grated sharp Cheddar cheese (½ pound)

The fastest hors d'oeuvre, chips, with an assortment of easy-to-put-together dips.

4 tablespoons (½ stick) butter or margarine
1 teaspoon Worcestershire sauce
1 package (8 ounces) cream cheese, softened
1 can (2¼ ounces) deviled ham

1 Combine Cheddar cheese, butter or margarine and Worcestershire sauce in a medium-size bowl; beat until fluffy. Blend cream cheese and deviled ham until smooth in a second bowl.
2 Pack each mixture into an about 2-cup size paper cup, smoothing top even. Chill both several hours or overnight.
3 When ready to serve, snip rim of each cup and gently peel off paper; invert cheese molds onto a serving plate. Frame with assorted crisp crackers.

Appetizer Cheese Spread

The perfect spread to serve with a selection of crisp, fresh vegetables

Makes 3½ cups

1 package (8 ounces) cream cheese
1 container (1 pound) cream-style cottage cheese
1 package (4 ounces) Camembert cheese
¼ cup grated Parmesan cheese
½ teaspoon seasoned salt
¼ teaspoon soy sauce
3 tablespoons light cream or table cream

(continued)

1 Beat cream cheese until smooth in a large bowl; beat in all remaining ingredients. Chill.
2 When ready to serve, spoon into a small serving bowl; garnish with sprigs of parsley or strips of pimiento, if you wish. Place bowl in center of a large serving tray; surround with crisp crackers, party-size breads, and carrot and celery sticks.

Tivoli Cheese Mold

Nippy blue and cream cheeses go into this zesty spread

Makes 6 servings

      1 envelope unflavored gelatin
      ½ cup cold water
      ½ cup light cream or table cream
      1 package (8 ounces) cream cheese
      ¼ cup crumbled blue cheese
      2 tablespoons chopped parsley
      ½ teaspoon salt
      ½ teaspoon paprika
      ½ teaspoon Worcestershire sauce

1 Soften gelatin in water in a small saucepan; heat over low heat, stirring constantly, until gelatin dissolves; remove from heat. Stir in cream.
2 Blend cream cheese with blue cheese in a medium-size bowl; stir in parsley, salt, paprika, and Worcestershire sauce; gradually blend in gelatin-cream mixture. Pour into a 2-cup deep mold. Chill several hours, or until firm.
3 When ready to serve, run a sharp-tip, thin-

blade knife around top of mold to loosen, then dip mold *very quickly* in and out of a pan of hot water. Invert onto serving tray. Garnish with a whole strawberry, if you wish.

Pecan Cheese Log

Stripes of pecans add a pretty trim and pleasing crunch to this zippy starter

Makes 12 servings

      1 package (8 ounces) cream cheese, softened
      1 cup grated Swiss cheese (4 ounces)
      1 cup crumbled blue cheese
      ½ teaspoon liquid red pepper seasoning
      ¼ cup chopped pecans

1 Blend cream cheese, Swiss cheese, blue cheese, and liquid red pepper seasoning in a

Two versatile dips that use sour cream and cream cheese, **Garlic Cheese Dip** and **Clam-Cream Dip**

medium-size bowl. Chill until firm enough to handle.

2 Shape into an 8-inch-long log; wrap in waxed paper, foil, or transparent wrap and chill again until firm.

3 To make spiral trim, unwrap log; press ½-inch-wide strips of foil or wax paper diagonally, 1 inch apart, over top and side. Roll log in chopped pecans; chill again.

4 When ready to serve, carefully peel off paper; place log on a serving plate. Frame with assorted crisp crackers, if you wish.

Rosy Hungarian Spread

The seasonings here are borrowed from the cuisine of Hungary

Makes about 1 cup

2 packages (3 ounces each) cream cheese, softened
2 tablespoons capers
1 tablespoon caraway seeds
1 tablespoon paprika
¼ cup dairy sour cream
½ clove garlic, crushed
1 teaspoon grated onion
¼ teaspoon liquid red pepper seasoning

Beat all ingredients with a fork or whirl in an electric blender until creamy-smooth. Use as a spread for rye rounds or crackers.

Pate Madrilene

Quick, easy, and not too expensive—but a classic

Makes about 3 cups

1 envelope unflavored gelatin
1 can (about 13 ounces) consommé madrilène
2 hard-cooked eggs, shelled
2 cans (about 4 ounces each) liver spread
½ cup chopped toasted walnuts
1 tablespoon sweet pickle relish, drained
½ teaspoon salt
¼ teaspoon pepper

1 Soften gelatin in madrilène in a small saucepan. Heat, stirring constantly, until gelatin dissolves; remove from heat. Pour a half-inch-thick layer into a 3-cup bowl; chill just until sticky-firm. Cool remaining gelatin mixture in saucepan at room temperature.

2 Cut up eggs, then press through a sieve into cooled gelatin mixture in saucepan; beat in liver spread, walnuts, relish, salt, and pepper until well-blended.

3 Pour over sticky-firm gelatin layer in bowl; chill several hours, or overnight, until firm.

4 When ready to serve, loosen pâté around edge with a knife; turn out onto a serving plate. Garnish top with sliced pimiento-stuffed olives, if you wish. Surround mold with crisp crackers.

NOTE: To toast walnuts, simmer in boiling water to cover in a small saucepan 3 minutes; drain. Spread in a single layer in a shallow baking pan. Heat in moderate oven (350°) 15 minutes.

Shrimp Salad Silhouettes

Tiny cutout of a contrasting color bread trims each two-bite sandwich.

Makes about 4½ dozen

1 can (5 ounces) deveined shrimps, drained, rinsed and flaked
¾ cup finely chopped celery
¾ cup mayonnaise or salad dressing
1 teaspoon curry powder
1 tablespoon lemon juice
14 slices white bread
14 slices whole-wheat bread
Butter or margarine

1 Mix all ingredients except bread and butter or margarine in a bowl.

2 Place 7 slices each white and whole-wheat bread flat on cutting board; spread with butter or margarine; trim crusts. With a knife, mark each slice into 4 triangles, then cut a small fancy design from each triangle; remove cutouts; place white ones in whole-wheat slices and whole-wheat in white.

3 Spread each of remaining bread slices with butter or margarine; trim crusts; spread with 2 tablespoons shrimp mixture. Put together with cutout slices; cut each into 4 triangles. Wrap and chill.

MAIN DISHES

Castillian Meatballs in Wine Sauce

For ground beef with a Continental flavor, try these meatballs that simmer in a wine-tomato sauce

Preparation time: 30 minutes.
Cooking time: 20 minutes.
Makes 8 servings.

- 2 pounds ground lean beef
- 2 large apples, peeled and shredded
- 2 eggs, slightly beaten
- 3 medium-size onions, chopped (1½ cups)
- 2 teaspoons salt
- ½ teaspoon pepper
- 2 tablespoons vegetable oil
- 1½ cups dry red wine
- 1½ cups water
- 2 cans (6 ounces each) tomato paste
- 1 teaspoon leaf basil, crumbled
- ½ teaspoon leaf rosemary, crumbled

1 Combine beef, apples, eggs, 1 cup of the onion, salt and pepper in large bowl; mix lightly. With wet teaspoon, shape into meatballs, about 1 inch in diameter.
2 Heat oil in large skillet; brown meatballs, half at a time, removing as they brown. Add remaining onion to skillet; sauté, stirring often, until golden. Stir in wine, water, tomato paste, basil and rosemary. Add meatballs; bring to boiling; cover; simmer 5 minutes.
3 Serve with buttered noodles and lima beans, as pictured, if you wish.

Beef and Eggplant Casseroles

Eggplant and meat sauce in a casserole that is ready to serve in less than an hour

Preparation time: 30 minutes.
Baking time: 20 minutes.
Makes 8 servings.

- 1½ pounds ground round
- 1 cup frozen chopped onion
- 1 large clove garlic, minced
- 2 tablespoons olive or vegetable oil
- 1 envelope (1½ ounces) spaghetti sauce mix with mushrooms
- 1 can (8 ounces) tomato sauce with cheese

- ¾ cup water
- ¾ cup dry red wine
- 1½ teaspoons leaf basil, crumbled
- 1 teaspoon leaf oregano, crumbled
- 1 medium-large eggplant, peeled and sliced (about 1 pound)
- ½ cup olive or vegetable oil
- ½ cup grated Parmesan cheese
- 1 pound mozzarella cheese, thickly sliced

1 Brown beef with onion and garlic in 2 table-spoons oil in a large skillet. Add spaghetti sauce mix, tomato sauce, water, red wine, basil and oregano. Cover; simmer, 15 minutes.
2 Sauté ½ of the eggplant slices in ¼ cup oil until limp and golden. Add remaining oil and eggplant slices. Transfer eggplant to 8 shallow oven-to-table baking dishes.
3 Spoon meat sauce over eggplant. Sprinkle Parmesan cheese evenly over casseroles. Top with thick slices of mozzarella.
4 Bake in a moderate oven (350°) for 20 minutes or until sauce bubbles and cheese melts.

Barbecued Chicken

This barbecue is done in the kitchen and not over the coals

Preparation time: 35 minutes.
Cooking time: 30 minutes.
Makes 8 servings.

- 1 cup flour
- 1 teaspoon salt
- 2 broiler-fryers, cut up (2½ pounds each)
- ½ cup vegetable oil
- 2 large onions, chopped (2 cups)
- 1 cup chopped celery
- 1 cup finely chopped green pepper
- 2 bottles (14 ounces each) catsup
- 3 cups water
- 5 tablespoons Worcestershire sauce
- 5 tablespoons brown sugar

1 Place flour and salt in a large plastic bag; add chicken pieces a few at a time; shake, coating chicken well.
2 Heat the oil in a large Dutch oven. Brown chicken pieces a few at a time. Remove pieces as they brown. Repeat, until all chicken pieces are browned.
3 Remove all but 2 tablespoons of fat from Dutch oven. Add onion; sauté until golden brown; add celery, green pepper, catsup, water, Worcestershire and brown sugar; stir well. Add

Some meals can be made the night before and heated up the following day;
Castilian Meatballs in Wine Sauce is one of these.

chicken to sauce, turning to coat chicken pieces. Cover. Cook slowly for 20 minutes, or until chicken is cooked through.

Chili Beans and Sausage

An easy-to-make, economical dish that will remind you of the Southwest

Preparation time: 25 minutes.
Baking time: 30 minutes.

Makes 4 servings.

2 pounds mild or hot sausage
2 large onions, chopped (2 cups)

4 cups peeled, diced tart apples
3 cups tomato juice
2 tablespoons brown sugar
2 cloves garlic, minced
2 teaspoons salt
2 teaspoons chili powder
1 teaspoon freshly ground black pepper
4 cans (15 to 17 ounces each) red kidney beans, drained
Dairy sour cream

1 Cook sausage just until it loses its pink color; break it up as it cooks. Pour off all the fat and cook onion in the same pan until it is limp. Add the apples, tomato juice, brown sugar, garlic, salt, chili and pepper. Bring to boiling; remove from heat. Add the kidney beans and stir to mix.

(continued)

3x9x2-inch baking dish.
moderate oven (350°) 30 minutes
til bubbly. Serve with sour cream.

NOTE: If you like a hot dish (as in spicy), use the hot sausage.

Incredible Beefburgers

These are so much more flavorful than ordinary hamburgers and take ground beef out of the "not *that* again" category

Preparation time: 20 minutes.
Cooking time: 14 minutes.
Makes 6 servings.

1 medium-size onion, chopped (1 cup)
1 tablespoon chopped green onion, tops only
1½ to 2 tablespoons butter or margarine
1 teaspoon dry mustard
½ teaspoon salt
⅛ teaspoon pepper
¼ teaspoon Worcestershire sauce
  Few drops liquid red-pepper seasoning
1½ pounds lean ground beef
1 egg, slightly beaten
  Vegetable oil

1 Sauté onion and green onion in butter or margarine until limp and golden in a large skillet. Add dry mustard, salt, pepper, Worcestershire and red-pepper seasoning.
2 Add beef and eggs; mix well, using your hands, if necessary.
3 For each 3 patties, heat 1 tablespoon of oil in a large skillet. Add patties and cook, over medium heat 4 to 5 minutes or until done as you like them.

Red and Green Pepper Steak

An impressive and tasty dish you make in minutes

Preparation time: 5 minutes.
Cooking time: 18 minutes.
Makes 6 servings.

2 medium-size green *peppers, halved, seeded and thinly sliced*
2 medium-size sweet red *peppers, halved, seeded and thinly sliced*

2 tablespoons olive or vegetable oil
1 chuck steak fillet (about 1½ pounds)
1 cup water
1 teaspoon Italian seasoning, crumbled
1 teaspoon salt
¼ teaspoon pepper

1 Sauté peppers in oil until soft in large skillet; remove to hot platter; keep warm.
2 Cook steak in oil remaining in skillet, turning once, 5 minutes on each side, or until steak is as done as you like it. Slice steak and arrange with peppers on hot platter.
3 Stir water, Italian seasoning, salt and pepper into skillet. Cook, stirring constantly, scraping to loosen cooked-on juices in skillet. Simmer 3 minutes to reduce volume by one-third. Pour over sliced beef and peppers. Serve with hot cooked rice, if you wish.

Jiffy Veal Tonnato

Convenience foods, and a blender help make this a quick-fix special

Preparation time: 35 minutes.
Makes 8 servings.

2 pounds ground veal
1 cup shredded carrots
1 cup dairy sour cream
1 small onion, chopped (¼ cup)
¼ cup packaged bread crumbs
1½ teaspoons salt
¼ teaspoon leaf thyme, crumbled
  Dash of pepper
2 tablespoons vegetable oil
1 can tuna (3¼ ounces)
½ cup dry white wine
1 tablespoon all-purpose flour
1 envelope or teaspoon instant chicken broth

1 Combine ground veal, carrots, ½ cup of the sour cream, onion, bread crumbs, salt, thyme and pepper in a large bowl; mix lightly until well-blended. Shape into 8 patties about ¾-inch thick.
2 Sauté in vegetable oil, turning once, until well-browned in a large skillet.
3 Combine tuna, wine, flour and chicken broth in container of electric blender; cover. Whirl until smooth. Pour over veal patties; cover.

4 Simmer, basting patties several times with sauce, 25 minutes, or until cooked through. Lift patties from sauce and place on a warm serving platter.
5 Stir remaining ½ cup sour cream into sauce; heat slowly just until hot. Spoon over patties.

Pork Chops Cacciatore

The short-cut here is spaghetti-sauce mix from your pantry shelf

Preparation time: 15 minutes.
Baking time: 1 hour, 15 minutes.
Makes 6 servings.

6 loin pork chops
1 large onion, sliced
2 tablespoons brown sugar
1 envelope spaghetti-sauce mix
2 cans (1 pound each) tomatoes

1 Brown chops in large skillet. Arrange in shallow 8-cup baking dish. Top with onion and brown sugar.
2 Blend sauce mix and tomatoes into pan drippings; bring to boiling; spoon around chops, cover.
3 Bake in a moderate oven (350°) 1 hour; uncover; bake 15 minutes longer, or until tender.

Ham Rolls with Curried Rice

Five ingredients—all from supermarket shelves —give you a dish to serve with pride

Preparation time: 20 minutes.
Baking time: 20 minutes.
Makes 4 servings.

1 package (6 ounces) curried-rice mix
2 packages (9 ounces each) frozen whole green beans
8 slices (about 1 pound) cooked ham, ⅛-inch thick
1 envelope white sauce mix
3 wedges process Gruyère cheese, cut up

1 Prepare rice mix following label directions; spread in a shallow 8-cup baking dish.

2 Cook green beans, following label directions; drain. Divide beans among ham slices; roll up slices. Place rolls, seam side down, on rice in baking dish.
3 Prepare sauce mix, following label directions. Add cheese; stir until melted. Pour over ham rolls.
4 Bake in a hot oven (400°) 20 minutes, or until sauce is bubbly.

Sausage-Spaghetti Bake

Layers of spaghetti and meat sauce make a hearty dish for family or friends

Preparation time: 40 minutes.
Baking time: 30 minutes.
Makes 6 servings.

1 pound sweet Italian sausages, sliced in 1-inch pieces
1 clove of garlic, minced
2 cans (about 1 pound each) stewed tomatoes
1 can (8 ounces) tomato sauce
½ cup water
1 teaspoon sugar
½ teaspoon mixed Italian herbs
1 pound thin spaghetti
½ cup grated Parmesan cheese

1 Brown sausages slowly in large skillet; push to one side. Add garlic and sauté 2 minutes; pour off all fat.
2 Stir in tomatoes, tomato sauce, water, sugar and herbs. Bring to boiling; lower heat. Simmer, covered, 30 minutes to blend flavors.
3 While sauce simmers, cook spaghetti, following label directions; drain well.
4 Spoon half of spaghetti into a 13x9x2-inch baking dish; top with half of meat sauce. Repeat with remaining spaghetti and sauce to make 2 layers of each; sprinkle with Parmesan cheese.
5 Bake in moderately hot oven (375°) 30 minutes, or until bubbly-hot. Let stand 5 minutes, then cut into 6 even-size servings. Lift out with wide spatula.

Sausage Pizza

With cheese, salami, and link sausages there is a good look to this tasty pizza

Preparation time: 10 minutes.
Makes 6 servings.

1 (12-inch) ready-to-heat pizza
6 slices provolone cheese (from an 8-ounce package)
6 slices salami (from an 8-ounce package)
6 smoked link sausages (from a 10- or 12-ounce package)
1 pepperoni (from a 5-ounce package)
Parsley

1 Place pizza on ungreased pizza pan or large cooky sheet. Cut cheese slices into quarters; cut salami and sausages in half; slice pepperoni into 18 rounds.
2 Arrange cheese quarters alternately with salami halves, spoke-fashion, on top of pizza to make 6 sections; place 2 sausage halves and 2 pepperoni rounds between each other near edge. Place 6 pepperoni rounds in a ring in center.
3 Heat, following label directions, or until cheese is bubbly-hot.
4 Place on large serving tray; cut into 6 wedges; garnish with parsley.

Walnut Chicken

There's a taste of the Orient in this easy-to-make skillet meal

Preparation time: 20 minutes.
Cooking time: 10 minutes.
Makes 4 servings.

¼ cup soy sauce
1 tablespoon dry sherry
½ teaspoon ground ginger
1 pound boneless chicken breasts, cut into 1-inch pieces
3 tablespoons vegetable oil
⅓ cup sliced green onion
1 garlic clove, cut in half
1 cup walnuts, coarsely chopped

1 Combine 3 tablespoons of the soy sauce, sherry and ginger in a medium-size bowl; add chicken pieces; let stand 15 minutes.

2 Meanwhile, heat wok or large skillet; add 2 tablespoons of the oil; heat until smoking; add green onion, garlic and walnuts. Cook 3 minutes, tossing mixture with slotted spoon; discard garlic. Spoon walnut-onion mixture into a small bowl; reserve.
3 Add remaining oil to wok; heat; add chicken pieces and soy mixture. Stir-fry until chicken is done and soy mixture begins to coat chicken, about 5 minutes. Add reserved walnut mixture and stir to mix. Serve with hot boiled rice, if you wish.

Clam Casserole

Here's the answer to a quick and simple meatless meal

Preparation time: 10 minutes.
Baking time: 30 minutes.
Makes 4 servings.

1 can (about 8 ounces) minced clams
Milk
6 tablespoons (¾ stick) butter or margarine
2 tablespoons all-purpose flour
1 egg
1 cup fine soft bread crumbs (about 2 slices)

1 Drain liquid from clams into a 2-cup measure; add milk to make 1½ cups.
2 Melt half of the butter or margarine in a medium-size saucepan; stir in flour. Cook, stirring constantly, until bubbly. Stir in the 1½ cups milk mixture; continue cooking and stirring until mixture thickens and bubbles 2 minutes; remove from heat; cool. Beat in egg and clams.
3 Melt remaining butter or margarine in a small skillet; stir in bread crumbs. Heat slowly, shaking skillet constantly, until crumbs are lightly toasted. Spoon half into a greased 4-cup baking dish; top with clam mixture; sprinkle with remaining buttered crumb mixture.
4 Bake in moderate oven (350°) 30 minutes, or until heated through.

Jiffy Shrimp Newburg

With shrimp from the freezer and soup from the cupboard, dinner can be ready in minutes

Preparation time: 15 minutes.
Cooking time: 8 minutes.
Makes 4 servings.

1 package (1 pound) frozen, shelled and deveined shrimp
1 can (10¾ ounces) condensed cream of
   shrimp soup
¼ cup milk
½ teaspoon salt
¼ teaspoon ground nutmeg
2 egg yolks
¼ cup dry white wine
   Hot cooked rice

1 Cook shrimp, following label directions.
2 Combine soup, milk, salt and nutmeg in a medium-size saucepan; bring to boiling.
3 Beat egg yolks slightly with wine in a small bowl; blend in about ½ cup of hot shrimp sauce; slowly stir back into remaining mixture in saucepan. Cook over low heat, stirring constantly, 1 minute, or until thickened; add drained shrimp.
4 Serve with rice; garnish with parsley and lemon wedges, if you wish.

Marinara Egg Scramble

Try this quickie for Sunday brunch

Preparation time: 5 minutes.
Makes 4 servings.

1 can or jar (1 pound) marinara sauce
8 eggs
¾ teaspoon salt
   Dash of pepper
¼ cup milk
2 tablespoons butter or margarine
4 slices white bread, toasted and halved diagonally

1 Heat marinara sauce until bubbly in a small saucepan.
2 Beat eggs with salt, pepper and milk until blended in a medium-size bowl.

3 Melt butter or margarine in a medium-size skillet; pour in egg mixture. Cook slowly, lifting mixture around edge as it cooks, just until eggs are set but still shiny-moist on top.
4 Place 2 toast triangles on each of 4 heated serving plates; spoon eggs on top; spoon marinara sauce over all.

Orange-Glazed Lamb Chops with Mint and Raisin Pilaf

A spiral of glistening lamb chops crowns a buttery pilaf flecked with peas, carrots and golden raisins

Preparation time: 12 minutes.
Baking time: 55 minutes.
Makes 4 servings.

8 rib lamb chops
½ teaspoon salt
¼ teaspoon leaf rosemary, crumbled
⅛ teaspoon pepper
2 tablespoons butter or margarine, melted
Glaze:
¼ cup tart orange marmalade
1 tablespoon vinegar
1 tablespoon bottled grenadine syrup
Pilaf:
1 cup frozen chopped onion
4 tablespoons butter or margarine
½ cup golden raisins
⅔ cup toasted slivered almonds
2¼ cups water
2 envelopes instant chicken broth
3 tablespoons frozen orange juice concentrate
1 tablespoon brown sugar
1 tablespoon dried mint flakes, crushed
⅛ teaspoon leaf rosemary, crumbled
¼ teaspoon bottled lemon-flavored salt
1 cup uncooked converted rice
1 package (10 ounces) frozen peas and carrots

1 Sprinkle lamb chops lightly with salt, rosemary and pepper, then brush with melted butter; arrange in a single layer on a broiler pan so that curved ribs all face the same way. Broil 5 inches from the heat 3 to 4 minutes until nicely browned.
2 Meanwhile, heat marmalade, vinegar and grenadine in a small saucepan until marmalade melts. Brush tops of broiled chops with glaze and let stand at room temperature while preparing pilaf. Keep glaze warm.

(continued)

3 Sauté onion in butter in a large skillet 3 minutes until soft. Add raisins, almonds, water, broth, orange juice, sugar, mint, rosemary and lemon-flavored salt. Simmer 2 to 3 minutes.

4 Stir in rice, bring to boiling; pour into a 12-cup paella pan or *au gratin* dish. Cover with foil. Bake in a moderate oven (375°) 20 minutes until rice is almost tender and most of the liquid absorbed. Add peas and carrots, tossing lightly to mix; arrange chops, browned sides up, in a spiral around edge of pan with rib ends pointing toward the center; brush with glaze.

5 Re-cover and bake 20 minutes; uncover, brush chops with glaze and bake 10 minutes longer.

Tuna, Artichoke and Mushroom Pot Pie

Hardly the usual tuna casserole, this biscuit-crowned, tarragon-scented pot pie is party perfect

> Preparation time: 15 minutes.
> Baking time: 25 minutes.
> Makes 6 servings.

¾ *cup diced celery*
1 *cup frozen chopped onion*
3 *tablespoons butter or margarine*
½ *teaspoon leaf tarragon, crumbled*
¼ *teaspoon leaf thyme, crumbled*
3 *tablespoons flour*
1 *can (3 ounces) sliced mushrooms*
¾ *cup light cream (about)*
½ *cup mayonnaise or salad dressing*
1 *tablespoon lemon juice*
1 *tablespoon dry vermouth (optional)*
½ *teaspoon salt*
⅛ *teaspoon pepper*
2 *cans (7 ounces each) tuna, drained*
1 *can (14 ounces) artichoke hearts, drained*
1 *package (8 ounces) refrigerated buttermilk biscuits*

1 Stir-fry celery and onion in butter in a medium-size saucepan, about 3 minutes until soft; blend in tarragon, thyme and flour; remove from heat. Drain mushrooms; pour mushroom liquid into a measuring cup and add enough light cream to measure 1 cup. Add to saucepan. Cook until thickened, about 3 minutes. Blend in mayonnaise, lemon juice, vermouth, salt and pepper; stir in mushrooms. Turn heat to lowest point and keep warm.

2 Empty tuna into a shallow 8-cup baking dish and flake with a fork. Add artichoke hearts, first halving or quartering any that are large. Pour in mushroom sauce and toss lightly to mix. Arrange unbaked biscuits on top of the casserole, not quite touching.

3 Bake, uncovered, in a moderate oven (375°) 25 minutes, or until biscuits are browned and tuna mixture is bubbly. Serve piping hot.

Baked Salmon and Green Bean Puff

Salmon and green beans, aromatic with dill, bake under a cloud of cheese soufflé for a casserole so showy no one will guess it's quick and easy to prepare

> Preparation time: 10 minutes.
> Baking time: 50 minutes.
> Makes 4 servings.

1 *package (9 ounces) frozen green beans*
2 *tablespoons water*
1 *can (1 pound) salmon*
1 *can condensed Cheddar cheese soup*
2 *tablespoons flour*
1 *tablespoon grated Parmesan cheese*
½ *teaspoon dillweed*
1 *tablespoon spicy brown prepared mustard*
1 *tablespoon minced drained capers*
1 *tablespoon caper juice*
⅛ *teaspoon pepper*
Soufflé Topping:
4 *eggs, separated*
¼ *teaspoon salt*
¼ *teaspoon dillweed*
  Pinch of pepper
2 *tablespoons grated Parmesan cheese*

1 Cook beans in water in a small covered saucepan over moderate heat, about 5 minutes until tender but still crisp.

2 Meanwhile, drain and flake the salmon, discarding any large bones or pieces of skin. Blend ¼ cup of the soup with the flour, then combine with the remaining soup; mix in grated Parmesan, dillweed, mustard, minced capers, caper juice and pepper.

3 Drain beans well and place in an 8-cup soufflé dish. Add salmon and cheese soup mixture; combine thoroughly. Bake, uncovered, in a moderate oven (375°) for 20 minutes.

4 When casserole has baked almost 20 minutes, prepare *Soufflé Topping*. Beat egg whites with salt to soft peaks; beat yolks with dillweed and pepper until smooth, then stir in grated Parmesan. Spoon a little beaten whites into yolk mixture, then pour yolks over whites and fold in gently until no streaks of white or yellow show. Spoon quickly on top of hot beans and salmon, return to oven and bake 30 minutes longer until puffy and touched with brown. Serve immediately.

Veal Parmigiana and Green Noodle Bake

Two Italian favorites team in this one-dish dinner

Preparation time: 15 minutes.
Baking time: 15 minutes.
Makes 4 servings.

1 package (8 ounces) green noodles
1 can condensed cream of mushroom soup
½ cup dairy sour cream
2 tablespoons milk
1 container (8 ounces) whipped cream cheese
½ cup grated Parmesan cheese
¼ cup (½ stick) butter or margarine, melted
1 can (3 or 4 ounces) sliced mushrooms, undrained
4 frozen breaded veal patties (about 1¼ pounds)
3 tablespoons butter or margarine
2 canned pimientos, slivered
1 package (8 ounces) mozzarella cheese
½ cup canned meatless spaghetti sauce

1 Cook noodles, following label directions.
2 Meanwhile, blend soup with sour cream, milk, cream cheese, Parmesan and melted butter; stir in mushrooms and their liquid. Set aside.
3 Quickly brown veal patties on both sides in butter in a large skillet. Drain on paper toweling; cut in half.
4 Drain noodles. Combine with soup mixture and pimiento; turn into shallow 12-cup baking dish. Arrange veal patty halves on top. Cut mozzarella into 8 slices; top each patty with one slice. Spoon spaghetti sauce in center of each cheese slice. Bake in a moderate oven (375°) 15 minutes, or until cheese melts. Garnish, with clusters of parsley or watercress, if you wish.

Pepperoni and Chick Pea Casserole

A robust Italian meal-in-one done the easy American way

Preparation time: 15 minutes.
Baking time: 1 hour.
Makes 6 servings.

2 pepperoni sausages, sliced thin
1 cup frozen chopped onion
½ cup frozen chopped green pepper
1 clove garlic, crushed
1 tablespoon parsley flakes
½ teaspoon leaf oregano, crumbled
¼ teaspoon leaf basil, crumbled
Pinch of salt
2 cans (8 ounces each) tomato sauce
½ cup dry red or white wine
2 tablespoons brown sugar
2 cans (1 pound, 4 ounces each) chick peas, well-drained
2 ounces Cheddar cheese, shredded (½ cup)

(continued)

1 Brown pepperoni lightly in a large skillet 2 to 3 minutes. Drain on paper toweling; pour drippings from skillet, then measure out 2 tablespoons and return to skillet. Stir-fry onion, pepper and garlic in drippings 3 to 4 minutes until soft and lightly browned. Mix in parsley flakes, oregano, basil, salt, tomato sauce, wine and brown sugar and let bubble, uncovered, stirring occasionally, 5 minutes.

2 Meanwhile, toss pepperoni, chick peas and cheese together in an 8-cup baking dish. Stir in skillet mixture.

3 Bake, uncovered, in a moderate oven (375°) 1 hour, stirring casserole once or twice as it bakes.

Polynesian Chicken Wings

Stir-fried vegetables and golden chicken wings are combined with a sweet-sour sauce. Spoon over crisp Chinese cabbage for a touch of Hawaii at home

Makes 4 servings.

12 chicken wings (2 pounds)
¼ cup all-purpose flour
1 teaspoon salt
¼ teaspoon pepper
¼ cup peanut oil
1 cup sliced green onions
   OR: 1 large onion, chopped (1 cup)
12 baby carrots, pared (from a 1-pound bag)
1 can (1 pound, 4 ounces) pineapple chunks
2 tablespoons lime juice or lemon juice
1 package (6 ounces) frozen Chinese pea pods, thawed (optional)
1 large red pepper, halved, seeded and cut into strips
1 cup sliced celery
1 cup sliced mushrooms
   Sweet Sour Sauce (see below)
   Shredded Chinese cabbage

1 Fold chicken tips up and under thickest joint. Shake in a plastic bag with flour, salt and pepper to coat wings evenly.

2 Brown chicken wings in oil in a large skillet; remove and reserve. Stir-fry green onion slices and baby carrots in skillet until glistening; return chicken wings to skillet; add ¼ cup pineapple liquid from canned cubes and lime or lemon juice to skillet; cover and simmer 15 minutes.

3 Add pea pods, red pepper, celery, mushrooms and pineapple chunks; toss to mix well; cover; simmer 5 minutes longer, or until

chicken wings are tender and vegetables are crisply-tender. Pour *Sweet-Sour Sauce* over and toss to blend well; spoon over shredded Chinese cabbage and sprinkle with chopped parsley. Or, sprinkle a handful of crunchy Chinese fried noodles over the top.

Sweet-Sour Sauce

You can have the flavors of a Polynesian restaurant at home, when you combine this sauce with chicken and vegetable dishes

Makes about 2 cups.

⅓ cup firmly packed brown sugar
3 tablespoons cornstarch
1 cup pineapple juice
3 tablespoons cider vinegar
3 tablespoons soy sauce

Combine brown sugar, cornstarch, pineapple juice, vinegar and soy sauce in a small saucepan. Cook, stirring constantly, until sauce thickens and bubbles 1 minute.

Brunswick Stew

This Colonial favorite goes modern with foods from the supermarket freezer

Bake at 375° for 45 minutes.
Makes 6 servings.

1 cup frozen chopped onion
¼ cup dry white wine
   Few drops bottled red pepper seasoning
1 can condensed golden mushroom soup
1 can (8 ounces) tomatoes
1 package (10 ounces) frozen okra, separated
1 package (10 ounces) frozen Fordhook lima beans, separated
4 ears fresh corn, cut into 1-inch pieces
   OR: 1 package (10 ounces) frozen whole-kernel corn, separated
1 package (1 pound, 12 ounces to 2 pounds) frozen fried chicken pieces

1 Simmer onion in wine and red pepper seasoning in a large saucepan 5 minutes; add soup and tomatoes; bring to boiling; add okra, lima beans and corn; return to boiling.
2 Combine frozen chicken pieces in a 12-cup casserole with vegetable mixture; cover casserole.
3 Bake in moderate oven (375°) for 45 minutes, or until bubbling hot. Serve with hot biscuits.

SANDWICHES

Mediterranean Medley

Men will go for this satisfying stack of shrimps, hard-cooked eggs and macaroni and olive salads on sliced rolls

Makes 4 servings

4 club rolls, each cut crosswise into 4 slices
⅓ cup bottled garlic salad dressing
  Bibb lettuce
1 container (1 pound) prepared macaroni salad
2 hard-cooked eggs, shelled and sliced
1 small cucumber, pared and sliced
½ cup olive salad (from a 12-ounce jar)
2 cans (5 ounces each) deveined shrimps, drained and rinsed
4 rolled anchovies (from a 2-ounce can)
  Potato chips

1 Place slices from 1 roll on each of 4 serving plates; drizzle with salad dressing; top with lettuce, then macaroni salad, spreading into an even layer to cover rolls.
2 Top macaroni with layers of sliced egg and cucumber, olive salad and shrimps; garnish with an anchovy. Serve with potato chips and additional salad dressing for everyone to sprinkle over top, if you wish.

Denver Sandwich

This has been a favorite for years and is worth renewing acquaintance

Makes 4 servings

1 small onion, chopped (¼ cup)
½ green pepper, chopped

3 tablespoons butter or margarine
6 eggs
6 tablespoons milk
  Salt and pepper
2 toasted, buttered, split hamburger rolls

1 Sauté onion and green pepper slowly in butter or margarine in medium-size frying pan 5 minutes.
2 Beat eggs slightly with milk and salt and pepper; pour into same pan; scramble with onion-green pepper mixture just until set.
3 Spoon onto hot toasted rolls.

Ham Bounty

Ham slices are rolled around tuna salad and whole green beans, then stacked atop white bread.

Makes 4 servings

2 cans (about 7 ounces each) tuna, drained and flaked
1 cup diced celery
2 hard-cooked eggs, shelled and diced
1 can (4 ounces) pimientos, drained and diced
½ cup coarsely broken walnuts
½ cup mayonnaise or salad dressing
½ teaspoon salt
1 can (1 pound) whole Blue Lake green beans, drained
4 tablespoons bottled oil-and-vinegar salad dressing
4 large oval slices white bread
4 thin slices Bermuda onion
12 long slices boiled ham (from three 5-ounce packages)
  Chicory or curly endive
  Preserved watermelon rind or pickle

1 Combine tuna, celery, eggs, pimientos, walnuts, mayonnaise or salad dressing and salt in a large bowl; toss lightly to mix. Chill at least 30 minutes to season and blend flavors.
2 Place beans in a shallow dish; drizzle with 2 tablespoons of the oil-and-vinegar dressing. Chill at least 30 minutes to season.
3 Just before serving, place each slice of bread on a serving plate; drizzle bread with remaining 2 tablespoons dressing; top with an onion slice.
4 Spoon ½ cup of the tuna salad onto each of 8 slices of ham; roll up, jelly-roll fashion. (Filling will hold rolls together.) Place two rolls on each slice of bread.
5 Drain green beans; roll inside remaining ham

(continued)

slices; place on top of tuna rolls. Garnish plates with a few sprigs of chicory and several pieces of watermelon rind or pickle.

Appian Sampler

Inspired by popular Italian antipasto, this sandwich combines a variety of food

Makes 4 servings

1 small loaf Italian bread, cut into 16 slices
⅓ cup bottled Italian salad dressing
  Romaine
4 medium-size tomatoes, each cut in 6 thin slices
2 packages (6 ounces each) assorted sliced cold cuts
4 slices provolone cheese, halved (from an 8-ounce package)
8 large fresh mushrooms, washed, trimmed and sliced thin
  OR: 1 can (3 or 4 ounces) sliced mushrooms, drained
12 small green onions, washed and trimmed
  Watercress
  Corn chips
  Red and green pepper strips

1 Place 4 slices bread on each of 4 serving plates; drizzle with salad dressing; top with romaine.
2 Layer bread this way: Tomatoes, meat, tomatoes, cheese, meat and mushrooms; lay 3 green onions across top of each sandwich. Tuck sprigs of watercress between layers or around edge of plates. Garnish plates with corn chips and pepper strips. Serve with ripe and stuffed green olives, and additional salad dressing, if you wish.

Change your sandwich habits with this exciting combination of tomatoes, cold cuts, provolone cheese, mushrooms, green onions, and pepper strips atop Italian bread, in **Appian Sampler.**

Serve **Cold Cut Roll-Ups** as an open-face or closed sandwich. Whichever way, you'll be delighted with the taste of the sandwich.

Cold-Cut Roll-Ups

Roll crisp coleslaw inside cold cuts and pile on big slices of zesty rye

Makes 6 sandwiches

1 small head cabbage (about 2 pounds)
2 tablespoons sugar
2 tablespoons mayonnaise or salad dressing
2 tablespoons light cream or table cream
2 tablespoons lemon juice
½ teaspoon salt
⅛ teaspoon pepper
½ cup (1 stick) butter or margarine
1 teaspoon prepared mustard
6 large slices rye bread
2 packages (6 ounces each) assorted Italian cold cuts
6 sweet yellow wax peppers

1 Shred cabbage into a large bowl. (There should be about 8 cups.) Sprinkle with sugar; chill at least 30 minutes.
2 Blend mayonnaise or salad dressing, cream and lemon juice in a cup; pour over cabbage. Sprinkle with salt and pepper; toss lightly with two forks to mix.
3 Blend butter or margarine with mustard in a small bowl; spread on bread.
4 Drain coleslaw. Spoon about ¼ cup on each slice of meat; roll up. Pile on bread, dividing evenly. Garnish each with a pepper.

Hawaiian Bologna Buns

Salad-style filling seasoned with soy sauce bakes inside crispy hard rolls.

Bake at 425° for 35 minutes.
Makes 4 sandwiches

4 large hard rolls
2 tablespoons butter or margarine
2 tablespoons instant-type flour
1 cup milk
2 teaspoons soy sauce
½ teaspoon curry powder
¼ teaspoon salt

¾ *pound bologna, cut in ¼-inch cubes*
1 *can (8¼ ounces) crushed pineapple, well drained*
¼ *cup sliced green onions*

1 Cut a thin slice across top of each roll and set aside for Step 3. Cut out centers of rolls to make shells. (Save centers to use for a crumb topper or croutons.)
2 Combine butter or margarine, flour and milk in a small saucepan; cook, stirring constantly, until sauce thickens and boils 1 minute; remove from heat. Stir in seasonings.
3 Mix bologna, pineapple and green onions in a medium-size bowl; stir in sauce. Spoon into rolls, dividing evenly; set tops of rolls over filling. Wrap each roll in foil.
4 Bake in hot oven (425°) 35 minutes, or until heated through.

Vienna Heroes

Little sausages and diced potatoes in a sweet-sour dressing make these hot hearties

Makes 6 servings, 2 rolls each

3 *cups diced pared raw potatoes (about 3 medium-size)*
1 *teaspoon salt (for potatoes)*
1 *cup water*
2 *cups diced celery*
1 *small onion, chopped (¼ cup)*
½ *cup diced dill pickle*
3 *cans (about 4 ounces each) Vienna sausages, cut into ¼-inch slices*
2 *tablespoons butter or margarine*
2 *tablespoons brown sugar*
2 *tablespoons cider vinegar*
2 *tablespoons water*
½ *teaspoon salt (for salad)*
¼ *teaspoon pepper*
12 *frankfurter rolls, toasted and buttered*

1 Cook potatoes with 1 teaspoon salt and water in medium-size saucepan 15 minutes, or until tender; drain. Mix in celery, onion and dill pickle
2 Sauté sausages, stirring often, in butter or margarine until lightly browned in medium-size frying pan. Stir in brown sugar, vinegar, water, ½ teaspoon salt and pepper; heat to boiling; pour over potato mixture; toss to mix well.
3 Mound salad mixture onto rolls, dividing evenly; serve hot.

Frankfurter Hobos

Grated Cheddar melts so invitingly atop hotdogs and creamy macaroni on onion rolls

Make 6 sandwiches

12 *frankfurters (1½ pounds)*
2 *cans (1 pound each) macaroni and cheese*
2 *teaspoons dry mustard*
6 *onion rolls, split and toasted*
Prepared sandwich spread
1 *package (4 ounces) shredded Cheddar cheese*

1 Place frankfurters in a large saucepan of boiling water; cover; remove from heat. Let stand 5 minutes, or until heated through; drain.
2 Mix macaroni and cheese with mustard in a medium-size saucepan; heat slowly just until bubbly.
3 Place toasted rolls, halves together, on a cookie sheet; spread with sandwich spread. Top each with hot macaroni mixture, then 2 frankfurters; sprinkle with cheese.
4 Broil, 4 to 6 inches from heat, 5 minutes, or until cheese melts and bubbles up. Serve hot.

Super Subs

Luncheon meat, eggs and cheese, along with peppy extras, make the salad filling

Makes 6 servings

3 *hard-cooked eggs, diced*
½ *can (12 ounces) pork luncheon meat, diced*
1 *package (8 ounces) process American cheese, diced*
2 *tablespoons mayonnaise or salad dressing*
2 *tablespoons pickle relish*
1 *teaspoon prepared mustard*
6 *frankfurter rolls, buttered*
Lettuce
Stuffed green olives
Radishes

1 Combine eggs, pork luncheon meat, cheese, mayonnaise or salad dressing, pickle relish and mustard in medium-size bowl; toss lightly to mix. (If made ahead, chill until serving time.)
2 Line buttered rolls with lettuce; fill with salad mixture, dividing evenly. Garnish with stuffed green olives and radishes threaded onto wooden picks, kebab style.

Twin Dagwoods on a Skewer

Each person gets two sandwiches—one with meats and the other with cheese.

Cut 1 long loaf of Italian or French bread in half, then cut each half into 8 slices, keeping them in order. Spread slices in pairs with softened butter or margarine. Fill first pair with sliced Muenster cheese folded around 1 or 2 thin tomato slices. Fill second pair with folded slices of bologna and salami tucked into romaine leaves. Repeat with remaining pairs, reforming loaf as each sandwich is made. Slip a thin slice of dill pickle between sandwiches; spear loaf with a long skewer to hold together. Makes 4 servings, 2 sandwiches each.

Supper Sandwich

A teenagers' delight, and a sandwich they can make themselves

Bake at 400° for 45 minutes.
Makes 6 servings

1 loaf Vienna bread, plain or with sesame seeds
  Melted butter or margarine
1 can (12 ounces) pork luncheon meat
1 package (½ pound) process Swiss cheese, grated
¾ cup mayonnaise or salad dressing
¼ cup sweet-pickle relish
1 tablespoon prepared mustard
1 teaspoon cider vinegar

1 Cut loaf into ¾-inch-wide slices almost through to bottom; brush cut sides with butter or margarine.
2 Mash meat with fork in large bowl; blend in remaining ingredients.
3 Spread meat mixture generously between slices (if bread is plain, brush top with melted butter or margarine and sprinkle with sesame seeds, if you wish); wrap loosely in aluminum foil; place on cookie sheet.
4 Bake in hot oven (400°) about 45 minutes, or until heated through.

When the gang turns up with a hearty appetite, take care of it easily with **Twin Dagwoods on a Skewer.**

Cheese Dreams

Easiest way we know to make a lot of sandwiches in a hurry

Bake at 500° about 5 minutes.
Makes 6 servings

½ cup (1 stick) butter or margarine, melted
12 slices white bread
12 slices process American cheese

1 Cut clean brown paper to fit a large cookie
sheet; brush generously with melted butter or
margarine.
2 Lay 6 slices bread in single layer on buttered
paper; top each with 2 slices cheese and another slice bread; cut in half; brush tops with
remaining melted butter or margarine.
3 Bake in very hot oven (500°) about 5 minutes,
or until tops are golden-brown and cheese is
melted.
4 Lift from paper with pancake turner; serve
piping hot.

Simple Salmon Jumbos

Layers of salmon salad, crisp cucumber, hard-
cooked egg, tomatoes and toast stack up to
this meatless hearty

Makes 4 sandwiches

1 can (about 8 ounces) salmon, drained,
boned and flaked
¼ cup mayonnaise or salad dressing
1 teaspoon lemon juice
¼ teaspoon salt
1 large cucumber, pared
12 slices white bread, toasted and buttered
2 medium-size tomatoes, sliced
4 hard-cooked eggs, shelled and sliced
4 large pitted ripe olives, each cut in 4 slices

1 Combine salmon, mayonnaise or salad
dressing, lemon juice and salt in a small bowl.
2 Cut a 2-inch-long piece from cucumber; set
aside for garnish in Step 4; slice remaining.

(continued)

There is no meat but plenty of goodness in **Simple
Salmon Jumbos.**

3 Layer each of 4 buttered toast slices this way: Salmon mixture, cucumber slices, toast, tomato and egg slices; top with remaining toast, buttered side down. Press wooden picks into sandwiches to hold in place; cut each sandwich diagonally into quarters.

4 Cut saved cucumber into matchlike strips; thread several through each olive slice; place on picks.

Champ

This is really a double-decker hero

Makes 2 or 3 servings

1 long loaf (about 16 inches)
  Italian bread
  Softened butter or margarine
6 slices (from 8-ounce package) process
  American cheese
6 slices liverwurst
1 dill pickle, cut into 8 thin slices
2 bottled hot red peppers, sliced
  Lettuce, olive oil, vinegar, salt
6 slices bologna
6 slices salami
1 tomato, cut into 6 slices
  Sweet onion rings

1 Cut bread into three lengthwise slices; spread cut surfaces with softened butter or margarine.
2 Cover bottom slice with cheese, liverwurst, pickle and hot red peppers; top with middle slice of bread.
3 Begin second filling with lettuce; drizzle with olive oil and vinegar and sprinkle with salt; top with bologna, salami, tomato and onion rings; replace crust.
4 Cut loaf crosswise into halves or thirds; wrap each in a paper napkin to eat out of hand.

Bologna-Cheese Kebab Sandwich

It's a little tricky to make, but this is a conversation piece when served

Bake at 350° for 20 minutes.
Makes 9 to 12 sandwiches

1 loaf Italian bread (14 to 16 inches long)
½ cup (1 stick) butter or margarine
4 teaspoons horseradish mustard

2 to 3 packages (6 ounces each) thinly sliced
  bologna (16 to 24 slices)
12 stuffed olives, sliced
1 package (6 ounces) cubed Cheddar cheese

1 Cut pointed ends from bread, then cut into ½-inch slices this way: Make first cut almost through to bottom of loaf and second cut clear through; repeat (finished individual sandwiches will be separate this way).
2 Cream butter or margarine with horseradish mustard; spread generously between the hinged slices; place 2 folded slices of bologna in each "sandwich," half in and half poking out.
3 Run two skewers (1 from each end) through bread to hold it together; place on a large piece of aluminum foil on cookie sheet; arrange sliced olives, then cubed cheese down center; bring foil up and around loaf and seal tightly.
4 Bake in moderate oven (350°) 20 minutes, or until heated through and cheese is melted. Unwrap; remove skewers before serving. Each sandwich will pull apart easily; serve hot.

Milwaukee Stack-Ups

Men will love these huskies of meat, sauerkraut and cheese.

Makes 6 servings, 2 sandwiches each

½ cup mayonnaise or salad dressing
½ cup tomato-pickle relish
12 slices round pumpernickel bread
2 cans (12 ounces each) beef luncheon meat,
  cut into 24 thin slices
12 long slices process Swiss cheese (about ¾
  pound)
1 can (14 ounces) sauerkraut, well drained

1 Mix mayonnaise or salad dressing and tomato-pickle in 2-cup measure; spread generously over bread slices; halve each slice.
2 Place 2 slices of luncheon meat side by side on each slice of cheese; top with a spoonful of sauerkraut; fold meat and cheese over sauerkraut and pop between 2 half bread slices. Repeat to make 12 sandwiches.

Dagwoods are stack-ups, with a generous filling between two layers of sandwich bread. Quarter them, and you'll find them easier to handle, and easier to enjoy.

Grilled Cheese for a Crowd

Count on this recipe for those times when a "hungry horde" arrives

Bake at 500° for 5 minutes.
Makes 12 servings

½ cup mayonnaise or salad dressing
¼ cup finely chopped dill pickle
24 slices white bread
3 packages (8 ounces each) sliced provolone cheese
½ cup (1 stick) butter or margarine melted

1 Mix mayonnaise or salad dressing and pickle in a small bowl; spread 1 rounded teaspoonful on each slice of bread.
2 Place cheese on half the bread slices, cutting cheese to fit; top with remaining bread, spread side down. Brush sandwiches lightly on both sides with melted butter or margarine; place on cookie sheets.
3 Bake in extremely hot oven (500°) 5 minutes, or until golden and cheese is melted. (No need to turn.) Cut in half diagonally; serve hot.

Melty Mix-Ups

Eat 'em hot right from their foil jackets

Bake at 400° for 15 minutes.
Makes 6 servings

1 can (12 ounces) pork luncheon meat
1 cup grated process Swiss cheese (half an 8-ounce package)

2 hard-cooked eggs, diced
¼ cup mayonnaise or salad dressing
1 tablespoon grated onion
½ teaspoon dry mustard
6 hamburger buns, split

1 Mash pork luncheon meat with a fork in medium-size bowl; stir in cheese, eggs, mayonnaise or salad dressing, onion and mustard.
2 Spoon into prepared rolls; wrap each in aluminum foil, sealing tightly; place on cookie sheet.
3 Bake in hot oven (400°) about 15 minutes, or until heated through.

Baked Puff Sandwiches

This is perfect for luncheon or a Saturday night supper

Bake at 350° for 45 minutes.
Makes 4 servings

1 can (12 ounces) pork luncheon meat
2 tablespoons bottled sandwich spread
8 slices slightly dry bread, buttered and crusts removed
3 eggs
2 cups milk
1 small onion, grated
1 tablespoon prepared mustard

1 Break up meat with fork; mix with sandwich spread; spread between bread slices to make four sandwiches; halve diagonally; arrange in single layer in shallow baking dish, 11x7x2.

(continued)

2 Beat eggs slightly in small bowl; blend in milk, onion and mustard; spoon over sandwiches; chill for at least 1 hour.

3 Bake in moderate oven (350°) about 45 minutes, or until top is puffed and golden; serve at once.

Meat Loaf Lineup

Flavorful meatloaf and seasoned bread combine in an unusual sandwich

Bake meat loaf at 375° for 55 minutes.
Makes 6 servings

1 *pound ground beef*
1 *egg*
1 *can (8 ounces) tomato sauce*
½ *cup fine dry bread crumbs*
1 *envelope (about 1½ ounces) spaghetti sauce mix*
1 *loaf Italian bread*
1 *teaspoon leaf oregano, crumbled*
6 *tablespoons (¾ stick) butter or margarine, melted*
1 *tablespoon grated Parmesan cheese*
1 *can or jar (4 ounces) whole pimientos, drained*

1 Combine ground beef, egg, tomato sauce, bread crumbs and spaghetti sauce mix in a

Accompany sandwiches with a hot, spicy drink.

medium-size bowl; mix lightly until well blended. Press into a loaf pan, 8x4x2.

2 Bake in moderate oven (375°) 55 minutes, or until crusty-brown.

3 Cut bread into 24 slices, keeping slices in order. Stir oregano into melted butter or margarine; brush over slices; put back in loaf shape. Brush outside of loaf with remaining butter mixture; sprinkle with cheese. Wrap loaf in foil. Heat in oven with meat loaf 10 minutes, or until hot.

4 Remove meat loaf from pan; cut into 12 slices; place 1 slice between each two slices of bread. Slit each pimiento down side to make two pieces; tuck alongside alternate slices of meat; tuck green-onion ruffles beside remaining slices, if you wish.

Butter-Crisp Herb Buns

A surprise ingredient—instant powdered cream—gives rolls a thin shattery crust

Bake at 350° for 20 minutes.
Makes 18 rolls

¼ *cup vegetable shortening*
½ *teaspoon ground nutmeg*
½ *teaspoon leaf oregano, crumbled*
¼ *teaspoon leaf basil, crumbled*
2 *packages active dry yeast*
¼ *cup warm water*
4¼ *cups sifted all-purpose flour*
¼ *cup instant powdered cream*
¼ *cup sugar*
2 *teaspoons salt*
2 *eggs, beaten*
1 *cup water*
3 *tablespoons butter or margarine, melted*

1 Melt vegetable shortening with nutmeg, oregano and basil in small saucepan; cool.

2 Dissolve yeast in warm water in large bowl; stir in cooled shortening mixture, 2 cups flour, instant powdered cream, sugar, salt, eggs and water; beat with wooden spoon; gradually beat in remaining flour to form a stiff dough.

3 Knead on lightly floured pastry cloth or board about 5 minutes, or until smooth and satiny; shape into a ball.

4 Place dough in greased large bowl; brush top with butter or margarine; cover with clean towel; let rise in warm place, away from draft, 1½ hours, or until double in bulk.

5 Punch down dough; turn out onto lightly floured pastry cloth or board; roll out to ½-inch thickness; cut out rounds with a 2½-inch cookie cutter; knead trimmings, roll and cut out to make

a total of 18 rounds; arrange in greased jelly-roll pan, 15x10x1;* brush with melted butter or margarine; cover with clean towel; let rise in warm place, away from draft, about 30 minutes, or until double in bulk.
6 Bake in moderate oven (350°) 20 minutes, or until golden-brown; turn out onto wire racks; serve hot.

* Or make only 9 buns with half the dough; bake in a greased square pan, 9x9x2. Shape remaining dough into a loaf; place in buttered loaf pan, 9x5x3; let rise 1 hour; bake 45 minutes, or until bread pulls away from sides of pan.

Frankfurter Bunwiches

Plump hotdogs, creamy coleslaw and rolls come ready-fixed—just put together and heat

Bake at 450° for 15 minutes.
Makes 8 servings

8 split frankfurter rolls
½ cup prepared sandwich spread
8 frankfurters (about 1 pound)
1 jar (1 pound) coleslaw

1 Spread rolls with sandwich spread; place a frankfurter in each, then spoon coleslaw on top, dividing evenly.
2 Wrap each sandwich in a square of foil; seal tightly. Place on cookie sheet.
3 Bake in very hot oven (450°) 15 minutes, or until hot. Fold foil back; serve sandwiches in wrappers.

Hot Steak Bunwiches

Flank steak is an easy cut to carve for sandwiches as it's all meat. Broil it fast for tender juicy perfection.

Makes 6 to 8 servings, 2 buns each

1 flank steak (about 2 pounds)
Salt and pepper
12 to 16 split BUTTER-CRISP HERB BUNS (recipe follows)

1 Make shallow diagonal cuts 1 inch apart on one side of steak (to keep meat from curling); place, scored side down, on broiler rack.
2 Broil, following range-manufacturer's directions, 3 minutes; turn; broil 3 to 4 minutes longer

for rare meat; season with salt and pepper; cut at once on the diagonal into thin slices. (If meat has to stand, keep slices close together, like uncut steak, to hold in juices.)
3 To serve, fold each slice in half, pop into a split hot bun.

DESSERTS

Pacific Pear Whip

The sky-high topping is simply whipped gelatin

Preparation time: 11 minutes.
Chilling time: 2 hours.
Makes 6 servings.

1 package (6 ounces) orange-flavor gelatin (family-size)
1 cup water
1½ cups ice cubes
1 bottle (12 ounces) ginger ale
1 can (1 pound, 1 ounce) pear halves, drained

1 Combine orange gelatin and water in a small saucepan; heat, stirring constantly, until gelatin dissolves. Pour into a medium-size metal bowl.
2 Stir in ice cubes and ginger ale until ice cubes dissolve. Place a pear half in each of 6 stemmed glasses or sherbet dishes. Pour ½ cup of gelatin mixture into each glass. (Don't worry if mixture is still foamy.)
3 Place bowl with remaining gelatin over ice and water and beat with electric mixer at high speed 2 minutes, or until gelatin triples in volume and holds the markings of the beater.
4 Spoon whipped gelatin over clear gelatin, swirling the last spoonful to make a pretty peak. Chill at least 2 hours before serving.

Orange Crown Mold

The refrigerator does the work for this spectacular dessert

Preparation time: 8 minutes.
Freezing time: several hours.
Makes 8 servings.

Chocolate-covered cream wafer sticks (from a 9-ounce package)
2 packages (2 ounces each) whipped topping mix
1 cup cold milk
1 can (6 ounces) frozen orange juice concentrate
2 tablespoons Curacao
Party candy patties (from a 9½-ounce package)

1 Line sides of a 6-cup mold or straight-sided dish with chocolate wafer sticks.
2 Beat topping mix and milk in a deep medium-size bowl with an electric mixer at high speed until mixture is thick and creamy; slowly beat in frozen orange juice and Curaçao.
3 Spoon into prepared mold; press mixture around wafer sticks. Cover mold with plastic wrap. Freeze 6 hours, or overnight.
4 Unmold by dipping mold into a pan of very hot water for a few seconds; invert onto serving plate and garnish with fruit-flavored party candy patties.

Fruited Grape Snow

Two-toned ring molds usually take several hours to make, but this treat is ready in practically no time at all

Preparation time: 11 minutes.
Chilling time: several hours.
Makes 8 servings.

1 envelope unflavored gelatin
1 cup white grape juice (from a 24-ounce bottle)
1 cup red grape juice (from a 24-ounce bottle)
1 package (10 ounces) quick-thaw frozen mixed fruits
1 package (3 ounces) lemon-flavor gelatin
1 cup ice cubes
2 egg whites
Red food coloring

1 Sprinkle unflavored gelatin into ¼ cup white grape juice in a small saucepan; let stand 5 minutes to soften. Heat gently, stirring con-stantly, until gelatin dissolves. Stir in remaining ¾ cup white grape juice and frozen mixed fruits until fruits thaw; spoon into a 5-cup ring mold.
2 Combine lemon gelatin and ½ cup red grape juice in a medium-size saucepan; stir over low heat until gelatin dissolves. Remove from heat; stir in remaining ½ cup red grape juice and ice cubes until the cubes have been completely dissolved; add the egg whites. Place saucepan in a pan of ice and water.
3 Beat with electric mixer at high speed until mixture thickens and doubles in volume; tint a pale pink with a few drops red food coloring; spoon over fruit layer in ring mold. Chill 6 hours, or overnight.
4 To unmold: Loosen mold around edges with a knife; dip mold *very quickly* in and out of a pan of hot water; shake mold gently to loosen; cover with serving plate; turn upside down; lift off mold. Garnish with clusters of grapes, if you wish.

Apricot-Cake Parfaits

Vanilla pudding becomes elegant in minutes

Makes 4 servings

1 package (about 4 ounces) vanilla pudding and pie-filling mix
1 jar (8 ounces) junior apricots
1 cup milk
4 ladyfingers
4 teaspoons apricot preserves
Whipped cream from a pressurized can

1 Combine pudding mix, junior apricots and milk in a medium-size saucepan; cook, following label directions for pudding. Cool completely.
2 Separate ladyfingers; spread half of each with 1 teaspoon of the apricot preserves; put back together. Stand each in the center of a parfait glass; spoon in cooled pudding. Chill.
3 Just before serving, garnish with whipped cream.

Ginger Peachy Shortcake

Packaged cake mix and pudding are the start of this summer meal-ender

Bake at 350° for 25 minutes.
Makes 8 servings

1 package loaf-size yellow cake mix
1 teaspoon ground ginger

Lovely to look at and just as scrumptious to taste, **Orange Crown Mold** is simple to make and because of the freezing time, perfect for a make-ahead dessert.

Egg
Water
1 package (about 4 ounces) instant vanilla pudding mix
1½ cups milk
1 cup light cream or table cream
½ teaspoon almond extract
6 large peaches, peeled, pitted, sliced and sweetened

1 Combine cake mix with ginger in a medium-size bowl. Prepare with egg and water, following label directions. Pour into a baking pan, 8x8x2.
2 Bake in moderate oven (350°) 25 minutes, or until top springs back when lightly pressed with fingertip. Cool 10 minutes in pan on a wire rack. Loosen around edges with a knife; turn out onto rack; cool.
3 Prepare pudding mix with milk, cream and almond extract, following label directions; chill.
4 When ready to serve, cut cake into 8 pieces; place each on a dessert plate. Spoon peaches over top. Stir pudding mixture until smooth; spoon over peaches.

Checkerboard Peach Cobbler

Refrigerated rolls make the topping for this easy dessert

Bake at 375° for 35 minutes.
Makes 6 to 8 servings

1 can (1 pound, 5 ounces) peach pie filling
½ cup firmly packed brown sugar
½ cup seedless raisins
½ teaspoon salt
½ teaspoon almond extract
1 package refrigerated orange Danish rolls with icing

1 Blend pie filling, brown sugar, raisins, salt and almond extract in a medium-size bowl; spoon into a baking pan, 8x8x2.
2 Separate rolls, following label directions; set container of icing aside for Step 3. Unwind each roll into a strip, then twist strip several times to make a rope about 8 inches long. Place 4

(continued)

of the ropes, spacing evenly, over peach filling in pan; place remainder crosswise over top to make a checkerboard design.

3 Bake in moderate oven (375°) 35 minutes, or until topping is golden. Spread icing thinly over top. Serve warm, with cream, if you wish.

February Shortcake

In spite of its name, this is a winner any month of the year

Bake at 450° for 15 minutes.
Makes 8 servings

2 *packages refrigerated buttermilk biscuits*
1 *cup sifted all-purpose flour*
½ *cup firmly packed light brown sugar*

½ *cup (1 stick) butter or margarine*
2 *packages (10 ounces each) quick-thaw frozen mixed fruits*
2 *firm ripe bananas*
1 *container (4½ ounces) frozen whipped topping, thawed*

1 Separate biscuits, following label directions. Place in a single layer in each of two 8-inch round layer-cake pans; press together to fill any holes and make an even layer.

2 Mix flour and brown sugar in a small bowl; cut in butter or margarine until mixture is crumbly. Sprinkle over biscuit layers.

3 Bake in very hot oven (450°) 15 minutes, or until firm and golden. Cool 10 minutes in pans on wire racks. Loosen around edges with a knife; carefully remove from pans.

4 While layers bake, thaw fruits, following label directions. Peel bananas; slice; combine with fruits.

5 Stack biscuit layers, shortcake style, on a serving plate with fruit mixture between and on top. Spoon part of the whipped topping in center. Cut shortcake into wedges; serve with remaining whipped topping.

The time may be seven o'clock, but it was only fifteen minutes earlier that **February Shortcake** was a collection of ingredients.

Apple Betty

Canned apple slices take all the work out of this old-fashioned standby

Bake at 375° for 30 minutes.
Makes 8 servings

2 cans (1 pound, 4 ounces each) pie-sliced apples, drained
½ cup firmly packed brown sugar
1 teaspoon ground cinnamon
¾ cup (1½ sticks) butter or margarine, melted
3 envelopes maple and brown sugar flavor instant oatmeal (from a 13-ounce package)
2 cups cubed bread (2 slices)

1 Combine apples, brown sugar and cinnamon in a large bowl; toss lightly to mix.
2 Drizzle melted butter or margarine over oatmeal in a medium-size bowl; toss with a fork until well blended; measure out ½ cup and set aside.
3 Add remainder to apple mixture with bread cubes; toss lightly. Spoon into a baking dish, 8x8x2; sprinkle the ½ cup oatmeal mixture over top.
4 Bake in moderate oven (375°) 30 minutes, or until puffed and golden. Spoon into dessert dishes; serve warm with cream or ice cream, if you wish.

Apple Crunch

Canned apples, pureed in the blender are layered with packaged buttery-rich cookies that have always rated high

Bake at 350° for 30 minutes.
Makes 6 servings

1 package (10 ounces) shortbread cookies
½ cup firmly packed brown sugar
1 can (1 pound, 4 ounces) pie-sliced apples, drained well
2 tablespoons butter or margarine
Cinnamon-sugar
Whipped cream from a pressurized can

1 Crush cookies fine. (There should be about 3 cups.) Tip to speed the job: Place cookies, half at a time, in a plastic bag and crush with a rolling pin.
2 Place crumbs in a medium-size bowl; stir in half of the brown sugar.
3 Place apples in an electric-blender container;

cover. Beat until smooth; pour into a medium-size bowl; stir in remaining brown sugar.
4 Press about one third of the crumb mixture over bottom of a greased baking pan, 8x8x2; top with half of the apple mixture. Repeat with another layer each of crumb and apple mixtures; sprinkle remaining crumb mixture over top. Dot with butter or margarine; sprinkle lightly with cinnamon-sugar.
5 Bake in moderate oven (350°) 30 minutes, or until firm and golden. Cool slightly in pan on a wire rack.
6 Cut cake into 6 serving-size pieces; top with whipped cream or your favorite custard sauce, if you wish.

Cheddar Pear Cobbler

Fruit and cheese for dessert in a superb baked dish

Bake at 400° for 25 minutes.
Makes 6 servings

6 tablespoons sugar
1 tablespoon cornstarch
¼ teaspoon ground nutmeg
1 can (1 pound, 14 ounces) pear halves
1 tablespoon lemon juice
1½ cups buttermilk biscuit mix
½ cup shredded Cheddar cheese
⅓ cup milk
Light cream or table cream

1 Mix 4 tablespoons of the sugar, cornstarch and nutmeg in a medium-size saucepan. Drain syrup from pears into a small bowl; stir into cornstarch mixture with lemon juice. Cook, stirring constantly, until mixture thickens and boils 1 minute; add pears. Heat very slowly while mixing topping.
2 Combine biscuit mix, cheese and remaining 2 tablespoons sugar in a medium-size bowl; stir in milk until mixture is moist, then beat 20 strokes.
3 Spoon pear mixture into a baking pan, 8x8x2; drop dough by spoonfuls in 12 mounds on top.
4 Bake in hot oven (400°) 25 minutes, or until topping is golden. Spoon into serving dishes; serve warm with cream.

Stuffed Pear Crumble.

With canned fruit on the shelf, desserts like this are a breeze

Bake at 350° about 30 minutes.

Makes 6 servings

1 can (1 pound, 14 ounces) pear halves
1 can (8¼ ounces) pineapple chunks
¾ cup (about 6 slices) zwieback crumbs
6 tablespoons brown sugar
½ teaspoon grated lemon peel
⅛ teaspoon salt
⅛ teaspoon ground nutmeg
2 tablespoons melted butter or margarine
2 packages (3 ounces each) cream cheese
5 tablespoons milk

1 Drain pears; place, cut side up, in baking pan, 8x8x2.
2 Drain pineapple chunks; save juice for Step 4; stuff pears with pineapple.
3 Blend zwieback crumbs, brown sugar, lemon peel, salt, nutmeg and melted butter or margarine in small bowl; sprinkle over and around pears.
4 Pour a little pineapple juice over crumbs; cover pan with foil.
5 Bake in moderate oven (350°) 15 minutes; remove foil; continue baking 15 minutes, or until crumb topping is toasty-brown.
6 Mash cream cheese with milk in small bowl; beat until smooth; serve over warm pears.

Pear Praline Cobbler

Refrigerated cookies add a special flavor and texture to a cobbler

Bake at 375° about 30 minutes.

Makes 8 servings

1 can (1 pound, 4 ounces) pineapple chunks
1 can (1 pound, 14 ounces) pear halves
½ roll refrigerated oatmeal cookies
¼ cup light brown sugar, firmly packed
1 tablespoon flour
MINT SPARKLE SAUCE (recipe follows)

1 Drain pineapple chunks and pears separately, saving syrups for making sauce.
2 Split the half-roll of cookie dough lengthwise; slice part into twelve ¼-inch-thick half-moons; press, rounded side up, around sides of a 9-inch pie plate.

3 Toss pineapple with half the brown sugar and all the flour in small bowl; spoon into pie plate, mounding in center; arrange pear halves, narrow end toward center, on top; crumble remaining cookie dough between pear halves; sprinkle pears with remaining brown sugar.
4 Bake in moderate oven (375°) 30 minutes, or until cookies are crisp and brown; serve warm or cold with MINT SPARKLE SAUCE.

Mint Sparkle Sauce

Makes about 2½ cups

½ cup sugar
3 tablespoons cornstarch
Syrups from canned pineapple chunks and pears
1 teaspoon lemon rind
2 tablespoons lemon juice

1 Blend sugar and cornstarch in medium-size saucepan; stir in fruit syrups (there should be about 2½ cups).
2 Cook over medium heat, stirring constantly, until mixture thickens slightly and boils 3 minutes; remove from heat; stir in lemon rind and juice; serve warm or cold.

Peach Melba Sponge

A pretty dessert you make quickly and let the refrigerator do the rest

Makes 4 servings

1 can (8 ounces) cling-peach slices
Water
1 package (3 ounces) raspberry-flavor gelatin
PINEAPPLE SAUCE (recipe follows)

1 Drain syrup from peaches into a 2-cup measure; add water to make 1¾ cups; pour 1 cup into a small saucepan. Dice peaches and set aside.
2 Heat syrup mixture in saucepan to boiling; stir into gelatin in a medium-size bowl until gelatin dissolves; stir in remaining syrup mixture.
3 Place bowl in a pan of ice and water to speed setting. Chill, stirring several times, just until as thick as unbeaten egg white. Keeping bowl over ice, beat vigorously with a rotary beater until mixture doubles in volume and mounds softly; fold in diced peaches. Spoon into a 6-cup mold. Chill several hours, or until firm.

4 Just before serving, loosen dessert around edge with a knife; dip mold *very quickly* in and out of hot water. Cover with a serving plate; turn upside down; gently lift off mold. Serve with PINEAPPLE SAUCE.

PINEAPPLE SAUCE—Combine 1½ cups pineapple juice and 1 package (about 4 ounces) vanilla instant pudding in a small bowl; beat, following label directions. Let stand several minutes to thicken. Just before serving, stir lightly. Makes 1¾ cups.
Note—Chill any leftover sauce to serve with plain cake or custard another day.

Cranberry Cream

Just five ingredients and minutes in the kitchen will give you this beauty

Makes 6 servings

1½ *cups bottled cranberry-juice cocktail*
1 *package (3 ounces) raspberry-flavor gelatin*

1 *package whipped topping mix*
Milk
Vanilla

1 Heat ¾ cup of the cranberry-juice cocktail to boiling in a small saucepan; remove from heat. Stir in gelatin until dissolved, then remaining ¾ cup cranberry-juice cocktail; pour into a medium-size bowl.
2 Place bowl in a pan of ice and water to speed setting. Chill, stirring often, just until as thick as unbeaten egg white.
3 While gelatin mixture chills, prepare topping mix with milk and vanilla, following label directions. Measure out about ½ cup and chill for garnishing dessert.
4 Beat thickened gelatin, keeping over ice and water, until foamy and double in volume; fold in remaining whipped topping mixture. Pour into a 4-cup mold. Chill at least 3 hours, or until firm.
5 When ready to serve, run a sharp-tip, thin-blade knife around top of dessert, then dip mold *very quickly* in and out of a pan of hot water. Cover with a serving plate; turn upside down; carefully lift off mold. Spoon saved whipped topping mixture in a puff on top.

Chocolate Velvet

Chocolate with a hint of almond plus cream adds up to this heavenly dessert

Makes 6 servings

⅓ *cup instant cocoa mix*
⅛ *teaspoon salt*
1½ *cups milk*
1 *envelope unflavored gelatin*
3 *eggs, separated*
½ *teaspoon almond extract*
¼ *cup sugar*
½ *cup cream for whipping*
¼ *cup flaked coconut*

1 Combine cocoa mix, salt and milk in a medium-size saucepan; sprinkle gelatin over top to soften.
2 Heat slowly, stirring constantly, until gelatin dissolves; remove from heat.

(continued)

It may look like a collection of hot dogs, but **Cranberry Cream** is a quick-fix dessert of cranberry-juice cocktail, gelatin, and whipped topping mix.

3 Beat egg yolks slightly in a small bowl; slowly stir in about ½ cup of the hot milk mixture, then stir back into remaining mixture in saucepan. Cook, stirring constantly, 5 minutes, or until mixture thickens slightly. Pour into a medium-size bowl; stir in the almond extract.

4 Place bowl in a pan of ice and water to speed setting. Chill, stirring several times, just until as thick as unbeaten egg white.

5 While gelatin mixture chills, beat egg whites until foamy-white and double in volume in a medium-size bowl; beat in sugar, 1 tablespoon at a time, until meringue stands in firm peaks. Fold into thickened gelatin mixture until no streaks of white remain. Spoon into a 4-cup mold. Chill several hours, or until firm.

6 When ready to serve, loosen dessert around edge with a knife; dip mold *very quickly* in and out of hot water. Cover with a serving plate; turn upside down; gently lift off mold.

7 Beat cream until stiff in a small bowl; spoon on top of dessert; sprinkle coconut over cream.

Double Raspberry Parfait looks great in individual-size cups or as a bowl-size dessert centerpiece.

Maple Cream

Smooth, light and just right for children or adults

Makes 8 servings

1 package (about 4 ounces) vanilla pudding and pie-filling mix
1 envelope unflavored gelatin
1⅓ cups water
½ cup maple-flavor syrup
3 eggs, separated
¼ teaspoon cream of tartar
¼ cup sugar
1 cup cream for whipping

1 Mix pudding mix and gelatin in a medium-size saucepan; stir in ⅓ cup of the water and syrup. Beat in egg yolks; stir in remaining 1 cup water.

2 Cook slowly, stirring constantly, until mixture thickens and starts to boil; pour into a medium-size bowl. Press a small sheet of wax paper on top of pudding. Chill about 1½ hours.

3 While pudding mixture chills, beat egg whites with cream of tartar until foamy-white and double in volume in a medium-size bowl; beat in sugar, 1 tablespoon at a time, until meringue stands in firm peaks. Beat ½ cup of the cream until stiff in a small bowl.

4 Fold meringue, then whipped cream into cooled pudding mixture until no streaks of white remain. Spoon into a 5- or 6-cup serving bowl. Chill several hours, or until firm.

5 Just before serving, beat remaining ½ cup cream until stiff in a small bowl; spoon in center of dessert.

Double Raspberry Parfait

Children will ask for this, again and again

Makes 4 servings

1 package (10 ounces) frozen raspberries
1 package raspberry flavor self-layering dessert mix
Boiling water

1 Thaw raspberries, following label directions; drain into a 2-cup measure. Add water to raspberry syrup to make 1⅓ cups. Spoon drained raspberries into 4 parfait glasses, dividing evenly and reserving 4 for garnish, if you wish.

2 Prepare dessert mix with boiling water, following label directions, then use syrup mixture prepared in Step 1 in place of cold water. Spoon over raspberries and chill at least 3 hours. Top with reserved raspberries, if you wish.

Coffee Tapioca

Instant coffee takes this old-fashioned dessert into a whole new world

Makes 4 servings

3 tablespoons quick-cooking tapioca
⅓ cup sugar
4 tablespoons instant coffee powder
⅛ teaspoon salt
1 egg, beaten
2¾ cups milk
½ teaspoon vanilla
¾ cup thawed frozen whipped topping

1 Mix tapioca, sugar, 3 teaspoons of the instant coffee powder, salt, egg and milk in a medium-size saucepan; let stand for 5 minutes.
2 Heat slowly, stirring constantly, to a rolling boil; remove from heat; cool. Stir in vanilla, then chill.
3 When ready to serve, spoon tapioca mixture, alternately with whipped topping, into 4 parfait glasses; sprinkle remaining 1 teaspoon instant coffee over tops.

Mocha Icebox Roll

Quick to make in the afternoon, and ready for eating at night

Makes 6 servings

½ pint cream for whipping
2 tablespoons cocoa (not a mix)
2 tablespoons sugar
1½ teaspoons instant coffee powder
1 package (8½ ounces) thin chocolate cookies
1 square unsweetened chocolate, grated

1 Combine cream, cocoa, sugar and coffee in small bowl of electric mixer; whip until mixture mounds softly.
2 Put chocolate cookies together with half the cream mixture in stacks of 4 or 5 cookies. Stand stacks on edge on serving plate to make one long roll. Frost outside with remaining whipped cream. Garnish roll with grated chocolate.
3 Refrigerate several hours. To serve, cut roll diagonally into slices.

Party Peach-Bowl Cheesecake

No one will ever guess how easily you turned out this beauty. Your secret: Cheesecake mix.

Makes 12 servings

2 packages cheesecake filling mix
3 cups milk
2 tablespoons lemon juice
¼ cup chopped candied orange peel (from a 4-ounce jar)
¼ cup chopped candied citron (from a 4-ounce jar)
¼ cup chopped toasted slivered almonds (from a 5-ounce can)
6 firm ripe peaches

1 Prepare cheesecake filling mix with milk, following label directions. (Save envelopes of graham-cracker–crumb mixture to make pie shells.)
2 Stir lemon juice, orange peel, citron and almonds into prepared filling. Spoon enough filling into 3-inch tart pan; spoon remainder into a 6-cup ring mold. Chill until firm.
3 When ready to serve, run a sharp-tip, thin-blade knife around top of large mold to loosen, then dip mold *very quickly* in and out of a pan of hot water. Cover mold with a shallow serving bowl; turn upside down, shaking dessert gently, if needed, to loosen; lift off mold.
4 Peel peaches, halve and pit. Save one half for center garnish, then slice remaining. Arrange part, petal fashion, around bottom of dessert. Spoon about ⅔ of remaining into center, then place the rest, petal fashion, on top. Place saved half, hollow side up, in center. Unmold cheesecake from tart pan; place upside down on peach half. Sprinkle with chopped candied orange peel, if you wish.

White Mountain Apricot Torte

This layered sweet stars thin pancakes made from a mix, golden jam filling, and quick fluffy frosting.

Bake at 450° for 5 minutes.
Makes 8 servings

2 eggs
1½ cups milk
3 tablespoons vegetable shortening, melted
1 cup pancake mix
GOLDEN APRICOT FILLING (recipe follows)
SNOW MOUNTAIN FROSTING (recipe follows)

(continued)

1 Beat eggs with milk and melted shortening in a medium-size bowl; stir in pancake mix, then beat just until smooth.
2 Heat a 7-inch frying pan. Test temperature by sprinkling on a few drops of water; when drops bounce about, temperature is right.
3 Pour batter,about ⅓ cup at a time, into pan, tilting pan to cover bottom completely. Bake 1 to 2 minutes, or until bubbles appear on top and underside is golden; turn; brown other side. Repeat with remaining batter to make 8 pancakes.
4 As pancakes are baked, spread with GOLDEN APRICOT FILLING and stack on an ovenproof plate; spoon SNOW MOUNTAIN FROSTING on top.
5 Bake in very hot oven (450°) 5 minutes, or until peaks of frosting are tipped with gold. Cut in wedges; serve hot.

GOLDEN APRICOT FILLING—Combine 1 cup apricot preserves (from a 12-ounce jar), 4 tablespoons (½ stick) butter or margarine, and ½ teaspoon rum flavoring or extract in a small saucepan. Heat, stirring constantly, just until butter or margarine melts.

SNOW MOUNTAIN FROSTING—Prepare 1 package fluffy white frosting mix, following label directions; fold in ¼ cup flaked coconut (from an about-3-ounce can).

Pink Lemonade Squares

Here's a real glamour dessert. Made with frozen lemonade mix, it's unbelievably simple.

Bake at 325° for 15 minutes.
Makes 9 servings

1 package (about 7 ounces) vanilla wafers
½ cup (1 stick) butter or margarine, melted
1 can (6 ounces) frozen concentrate for pink lemonade
¾ cup water
48 marshmallows (from a 10-ounce bag or 3 four-ounce packages)
1 cup cream for whipping

1 Crush vanilla wafers fine between sheets of wax paper with rolling pin. (There should be about 2 cups crumbs.)
2 Mix crumbs and melted butter or margarine in a medium-size bowl; measure out ½ cup and set aside for topping in Step 5. Press remaining evenly in bottom and halfway up sides of a baking dish, 8x8x2. (Crumbs will make a thick layer that bakes into a candylike crust.)
3 Bake in slow oven (325°) 15 minutes; cool completely on wire rack.
4 Combine concentrate for lemonade and water in a medium-size saucepan; heat slowly until

Two dessert lovelies that are quick to put together and are bitingly good on the taste buds, **Party Peach-Bowl Cheese-Cake** (rear), **White Mountain Apricot Torte** (right), look good on any table.

lemonade thaws and mixture is hot. Add marsh-mallows; continue heating, stirring constantly, just until marshmallows melt and mixture is smooth. Chill several hours, or until syrupy-thick.

5 Beat cream until stiff in a medium-size bowl; fold into marshmallow mixture until no streaks of white remain. Spoon into cooled crust; sprinkle saved crumbs over.

6 Freeze several hours, or until firm. Cut into squares; serve plain or top with additional whipped cream, if you wish. Dessert cuts neater if allowed to stand at room temperature about 30 minutes before serving.

Frozen Venetian Parfait

Make this in minutes, freeze it, and enjoy a continental dessert

Makes 4 servings

½ cup marshmallow cream
1 tablespoon water
1 pint vanilla ice cream, softened
½ cup ground almonds
2 tablespoons chopped candied red cherries
1 teaspoon grated orange peel

1 Line a 3-cup mixing bowl with foil, allowing an overhang of 1 inch.
2 Combine marshmallow cream with water in a medium-size bowl; stir until well blended; beat in ice cream; stir in almonds, cherries and orange peel. Spoon into lined bowl; cover.
3. Freeze overnight or until firm. To unmold: Invert bowl on serving plate; pull out parfait by foil overhang; peel off foil. Decorate with candied cherry halves, if you wish.

Peach Tortoni

Bits of fruit and crunchy cookie crumbs blend with almond cream in this ice-cream–style treat.

Makes 6 servings

1 package (10 ounces) frozen sliced peaches, thawed and mashed
12 crisp macaroon cookies (from a 10-ounce package), coarsely crushed
½ cup cream for whipping
4 tablespoons 10X (confectioners' powdered) sugar
¼ teaspoon almond extract

1 Combine peaches and crushed macaroons.
2 Beat cream with 10X sugar and almond extract until stiff; fold into peach mixture.
3 Spoon into 6 individual foil or double-thick paper baking cups; set on a small tray or cookie sheet for easy handling. Wrap, label, date and freeze.
4 About ½ hour before serving time, remove from freezer and let stand at room temperature to soften slightly. Serve right in the cups.

Royal Grape Parfait

This regal-looking dessert goes together fast and freezes into an inviting mauve color.

Makes 6 servings

2 cups cream for whipping
¼ cup sifted 10X (confectioners' powdered) sugar
1 can (6 ounces) frozen concentrated grape juice, thawed
1 teaspoon vanilla

1 Beat cream and 10X sugar until stiff in a medium-size bowl; gradually fold in thawed grape juice and vanilla.
2 Spoon into a 5-cup mold or 2 ice-cube trays; freeze at least 2 hours, or until creamy-firm. Serve in parfait glasses.

Cheese Cake Hawaiian

A superb refrigerator cheese cake with a touch from the Islands

Bake at 350° for 10 minutes.
Makes 12 servings

1 cup vanilla wafer crumbs
2 tablespoons sugar (for crust)
2 tablespoons melted butter or margarine
1 package (6 ounces) lemon-flavor gelatin
1 cup boiling water
3 eggs, separated
1 container (1 pound) cream-style cottage cheese
2 teaspoons vanilla
¼ teaspoon ground cardamom
½ cup sugar (for filling)
Hawaiian Topping (recipe follows)

1 Combine crumbs with the 2 tablespoons sugar in a medium-size bowl; blend in melted
(continued)

butter or margarine. Press evenly over bottom and side of a buttered 8-inch spring-form pan.
2 Bake in moderate oven (350°) 10 minutes, or until crumbs are set. Cool while making filling.
3 Dissolve gelatin in boiling water in a medium-size saucepan. Beat egg yolks slightly in a small bowl. Slowly stir half of hot gelatin mixture into beaten eggs; stir back into pan. Cook until mixture thickens slightly.
4 Sieve cottage cheese into a large bowl; blend in gelatin mixture, vanilla, and cardamom. Chill until thickened.
5 Beat egg whites until foamy-white and double in volume in a small bowl. Beat in the ½ cup sugar, 1 tablespoon at a time, until meringue stands in firm peaks. Fold into cottage cheese mixture. Pour into prepared crumb crust. Chill 4 hours, or until firm.
6 Loosen cake around edge with a knife; release spring and carefully lift off side of pan. Slide cake, still on metal base, onto a serving plate. Top with *Hawaiian Topping* . Chill 1 hour, or until serving time.

HAWAIIAN TOPPING—Drain the syrup from 1 eight-ounce can sliced pineapple into a small saucepan; blend in 2 teaspoons cornstarch. Cook, stirring constantly, until mixture thickens and bubbles 3 minutes. Stir in 2 tablespoons syrup from maraschino cherries; cool slightly. Arrange pineapple slices and 4 maraschino cherries on top of cheese cake. Brush glaze over fruits and cheese cake.

Apricot Creams

Dried fruits make the nicest bite-size sweets—like little no-cook candies.

Makes about 5 dozen

½ cup golden raisins
½ cup toasted slivered almonds
1 cup 10X (confectioners' powdered) sugar
2 tablespoons dairy sour cream
1 package (11 ounces) dried apricot halves

1 Chop raisins and almonds; blend with 10X sugar and sour cream in a small bowl.
2 Separate apricot halves; spoon a scant teaspoonful raisin mixture in center of each half. Chill.

ICE CREAM, SHERBERT, ICE

For a quick end-of-the-meal treat, serve ice cream, sherbert, or ice. Except for the ice, they provide another of the day's daily milk requirements. Keep them handy for those instant moments. Here's a dictionary of the most popular.

Ice Cream. *This owes its smoothness to a blending of milk, cream, sweetening, and flavoring. "Premium" on the carton means that the ice cream contains extra milk fat and higher-quality ingredients. It usually has less air whipped in.*

French Ice Cream or French Custard Ice Cream. *Either of these contains more egg or egg yolks than other frozen desserts.*

Diabetic or Dietetic Ice Cream. *Exact recipes vary from state to state, but all are artificially sweetened.*

Mellorine. *Available in a few areas, this looks and tastes like ice cream but is made with vegetable or animal fat instead of butter fat.*

Ice Milk. *It contains fewer milk solids, but usually more sugar than ice cream: ½ cup vanilla ice milk = 152 calories; the same amount of vanilla ice cream = 193 calories.*

Soft-Frozen Dairy Dessert. *Often called frozen custard, it is creamy-soft and smooth.*

Sherbet. *Recipes combine dairy ingredients, sweetening, fruit or juice, and fruit acid.*

Ice. *This is a non-dairy food. It is made of water, sugar, and fruit or juice.*

Spumoni. *An Italian specialty, it has an outer layer of vanilla ice cream and a center of chocolate, fruit, or macaroon mousse.*

Tortoni. *Another Italian treat. To the ice cream extra cream is added. The mixture is frozen in individual molds and topped with macaroon crumbs.*

Frozen Yogurt. *Fast gaining popularity, this is a fermented, custardlike milk product having a tangy flavor. It is made from fresh, partially skimmed, cow's milk.*

Raspberry Mousse Cookie Pie

Packaged cookies make this quick-as-a-wink crust

Makes 6 servings

    1 package (16 ounces) frozen raspberries,
      thawed
    1 package (3 ounces) raspberry-flavor gelatin
    1 cup hot water
   16 marshmallows (¼ pound)
   24 lemon-wafer cookies
    1 cup cream for whipping
      Brazil-nut curls

1 Drain raspberries; set berries aside for Step 5; combine juice, gelatin and hot water in medium-size saucepan; stir until gelatin dissolves.
2 Add marshmallows; cook over medium heat, stirring often, until marshmallows melt completely; pour into large bowl; chill until mixture is thick and syrupy.
3 While gelatin chills, line bottom and sides of a 9-inch pie plate with cookies.
4 Beat thickened gelatin with rotary beater (this takes lots of beating) or in an electric mixer until it doubles in bulk, turns light pink, and mounds slightly when dropped from a spoon.
5 Fold in raspberries very gently; if mixture gets too soft, chill a few minutes.
6 Beat cream until stiff; fold gently into raspberry mixture; spoon into cookie crust; chill until set; garnish with Brazil-nut curls made by shaving thin slices with vegetable parer from moist nuts.

Pumpkin Tarts

Tiny pies made with custard mix for the smooth richness you like; packaged tart shells for extra ease.

Makes 6 tarts

    1 package (about 3 ounces) egg custard mix
    1 egg yolk
    ¼ cup sugar
    1 can (1 pound) pumpkin
   1½ teaspoons pumpkin-pie spice
    1 cup milk
    ¼ cup orange juice
    1 package (6 to a package) graham-cracker
      tart shells
      Whipped topping from a pressurized can

1 Combine custard mix, egg yolk, sugar, pumpkin, spice, milk and orange juice in a me-

Small in size but big on taste, **Pumpkin Tarts** start off with packaged tart shells for speedy serving.

dium-size saucepan. Heat slowly, stirring constantly, to boiling; remove from heat. Cool slightly.
2 Spoon into tart shells. Chill at least 2 hours, or until softly set.
3 Just before serving, garnish each with whipped topping and a canned mandarin-orange segment, if you wish.

Napoleon Creams

From refrigerated rolls and pudding mix comes a fine facsimile of a great traditional pastry.

Bake at 375° for 13 minutes.
Makes 8 pastries

    1 package (about 3 ounces) vanilla pudding
      and pie-filling mix
    2 egg yolks
    1 cup milk
    1 package refrigerated crescent dinner rolls
    1 cup cream for whipping
    1 cup - sifted 10X (confectioners' powdered)
      sugar
    2 tablespoons water
    1 envelope (1 ounce) liquid unsweetened
      chocolate

1 Place pudding mix in a medium-size saucepan; beat in egg yolks and milk. Cook, following label directions. Pour into a medium-size bowl; chill.
2 While pudding chills, separate crescent-roll dough into 4 rectangles; pinch together at perforations. Place rectangles on a large cookie sheet.
3 Bake in moderate oven (375°) 13 minutes,

(continued)

or until puffed and lightly golden; remove to wire racks; cool completely. Trim edges of rectangles to straighten, then cut each into three 2-inch-wide pieces with a sharp knife; split each piece to make 2 thin layers.

4 Beat cream until stiff in a medium-size bowl; fold into chilled pudding. Spread over 16 of the pastry rectangles; stack in pairs; top each with a plain rectangle. Place on a wire rack set over wax paper.

5 Blend 10X sugar and water until smooth in a small bowl; spoon over rectangles to glaze lightly.

6 Snip a small hole in one corner of envelope of chocolate; slowly drizzle chocolate in parallel lines over glaze. Using a wooden pick, draw across lines to pull chocolate to make tiny squares. Chill desserts until serving time.

Orange Walnut Cake

In next to no time, this show-off cake is ready

Bake at 350° for 50 minutes.
Makes an 8-inch round cake

1 package yellow cake mix
2 teaspoons grated orange peel
½ cup orange juice
¾ cup water
½ cup finely chopped walnuts
    ORANGE GLAZE (recipe follows)

1 Grease an 8-inch spring-form pan; flour lightly, tapping out any excess.

2 Combine cake mix, orange peel and juice and water in a large bowl; beat, following label directions; stir in walnuts. Pour into prepared pan.

3 Bake in moderate oven (350°) 50 minutes, or until top springs back when lightly pressed with fingertip. Cool in pan on a wire rack 10 minutes. Loosen cake around edge with a knife; release spring and carefully lift off side of pan. Place cake on a wire rack; cool completely. Remove cake from metal base; place on a serving plate.

4 Make ORANGE GLAZE. Spoon over top of cake, letting mixture drizzle down side. Sprinkle thin strips of orange peel over top, if you wish.

ORANGE GLAZE—Blend 1 cup sifted 10X (confectioners' powdered) sugar and 1 tablespoon orange juice until smooth in a small bowl; stir in 1 tablespoon more orange juice, part at a time, until glaze is thin enough to pour from a spoon.

Old-Fashioned Spice Cake

A can of tomato soup is the magic ingredient

Bake at 350° for 30 minutes.
Makes an 8-inch double-layer cake

2 cups sifted all-purpose flour
1 teaspoon baking powder
1 teaspoon baking soda
1 teaspoon ground cinnamon
¼ teaspoon ground nutmeg
¼ teaspoon salt
4 tablespoons (½ stick) butter or margarine
1 cup sugar
1 egg
1 can (10¾ ounces) condensed tomato soup
½ cup chopped walnuts
½ cup golden raisins
    LEMON-BUTTER FROSTING (recipe follows)

1 Grease two 8x1½-inch round layer-cake pans; flour lightly, tapping out any excess.

2 Sift flour, baking powder, soda, cinnamon, nutmeg and salt onto wax paper.

3 Cream butter or margarine with sugar until fluffy in a large bowl; beat in egg.

4 Beat in flour mixture, half at a time, alternately with tomato soup, beating just until blended. Stir in walnuts and raisins. Pour into prepared pans.

5 Bake in moderate oven (350°) 30 minutes, or until centers spring back when lightly pressed with fingertip. Cool in pans on wire racks 10 minutes. Loosen around edges with a knife; turn out onto racks; cool completely.

6 Fill and frost, layer-cake style, with LEMON-BUTTER FROSTING.

LEMON-BUTTER FROSTING—Cream 4 tablespoons (½ stick) butter or margarine with 1 cup sifted 10X (confectioners' powdered) sugar in a large bowl; stir in 1 tablespoon lemon juice. Beat in 1 cup more 10X sugar, alternately with 2 teaspoons milk, until smooth and easy to spread. Makes about 1¼ cups.

Banana-Lemon Torte

Layer upon layer of mix-made banana cake, with fresh fruit slices and creamy lemon frosting in between

Bake cake at 350° for 30 to 35 minutes.
Makes one 9-inch torte

1 package banana cake mix
    Eggs
    Water

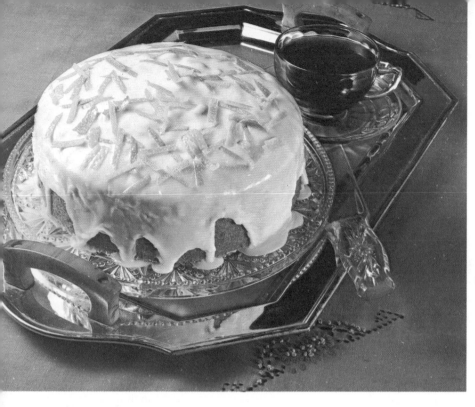

Orange Walnut Cake is not for tomorrow. Mix it when you are quick-fixing your main dish, and cook. By the time you are ready for dessert the cake is ready for you.

1 package lemon-flavor creamy frosting mix
2 cups cream for whipping
3 medium-size bananas
　Lemon juice

1 Prepare cake mix with eggs and water, bake in 2 greased-and-floured 9x1½-inch layer-cake pans, cool, and remove from pans, following label directions. Split each layer.
2 Blend frosting mix and cream in a medium-size bowl; beat until fluffy-thick.
3 Peel bananas and slice thin; brush with lemon juice so slices stay bright.
4 Place one cake layer on a large serving plate; spread with about ¼ of the frosting mixture; top with ¼ of the banana slices. Repeat stacking with remaining layers, frosting mixture and banana slices, arranging banana slices in a pretty pattern on top. Chill torte about an hour before serving. Cut in wedges with a sharp knife.

Ribbons

Striped with tinted frostings, these three-layer gems look so colorful

Bake at 325° for 20 minutes.
Makes 40 cakes

1 package pound cake mix
　Milk
　Eggs
½ teaspoon almond extract

1 cup vanilla frosting (from a 1-pound, 5-ounce can)
　Red, green and yellow food colorings

1 Line three baking pans, 9x9x2, with wax paper; grease paper.
2 Prepare pound cake mix with milk and eggs, following label directions; divide evenly into prepared pans.
3 Bake in slow oven (325°) 20 minutes, or until a wooden pick inserted in tops comes out clean. Cool in pans on a wire rack 5 minutes; remove from pans; peel off wax paper. Cool completely.
4 Stir almond extract into frosting in a bowl; divide in thirds. Tint one pink, one green and one yellow with food colorings. Spread each on a cake layer; stack layers. Chill. Cut into eighths crosswise, then fifths lengthwise. Trim with frosting rosettes, if you wish.

Rocky Road Roll-up

With a little sleight-of-hand, packaged jelly roll goes homemade fancy in mere minutes

Bake at 400° for 10 minutes.
Makes 6 servings

1 can (about 1 pound, 6 ounces) pineapple pie filling
1 packaged jelly roll
¼ cup semi-sweet chocolate pieces

(continued)

1 Place pineapple pie filling in a sieve set in a bowl; lift and turn filling over and over with a rubber spatula until most of the thick juice has drained off.
2 Unroll jelly roll; spread evenly with the drained fruit to within ½ inch of edges. Reroll carefully; place, seam side down, on a greased cookie sheet. Brush all over with the thickened juice from pie filling.
3 Bake in hot oven (400°) 10 minutes, or until glaze bubbles; remove roll from oven. Dot top at once with semisweet-chocolate pieces.
4 Lift roll onto a serving plate. Slice and serve warm with vanilla ice cream, if you wish.

Ticktacktoe Jewel Cake

A three-layer cake and, surprise, the middle one is a fruit gelatin mixture

Makes 8 servings

1 can (about 1 pound) fruit cocktail
1 package (3 ounces) strawberry-flavor gelatin
1 cup boiling water
1 nine-inch yellow cake layer
2½ cups thawed frozen whipped topping (from a 9-ounce container)

1 Drain syrup from fruit cocktail into a cup.
2 Dissolve gelatin in boiling water in a medium-size bowl; stir in ½ cup of the fruit syrup. Measure ¼ cup of the mixture into a small shallow pan or dish to make a thin layer. Chill until firm for garnish.
3 Chill remaining gelatin mixture 30 minutes, or until as thick as unbeaten egg white; fold in fruit cocktail. Spoon into an 8-inch round layer-cake pan. Chill several hours, or until firm. Place a piece of transparent wrap or foil over a large flat plate. Loosen gelatin layer around edge with a knife; dip pan *very quickly* in and out of hot water; turn out onto wrapped plate. Split cake layer; spread each half with ¼ cup of the whipped topping; place half, spread side down, over gelatin layer. Cover with a serving plate; turn upside down; lift off plate and peel off paper. Place remaining cake layer, spread side down, over gelatin.
Frost side and top of cake with about two thirds of the remaining whipped topping. Press remainder through a pastry bag in ribbons to form blocks on top of cake and rosettes at edge.
Cut the ¼ cup gelatin mixture into tiny cubes; spoon into blocks on cake. Chill until serving time.

Walnut Sticks

Make these from piecrust mix; they will be a hit and the cookie jar will empty fast

Bake at 425° for 7 minutes.
Makes about 5 dozen

1 package piecrust mix
¼ cup apricot nectar
⅓ cup very finely chopped walnuts
3 tablespoons sugar
¾ teaspoon ground cinnamon

1 Prepare piecrust mix with apricot nectar instead of water, following label directions; divide in half. Roll out, half at a time, on a lightly floured pastry cloth or board to a rectangle about 13x8; trim edges even to make a rectangle, 12x7.
2 Mix walnuts, sugar and cinnamon in a small bowl; sprinkle half over each pastry rectangle; press in firmly with rolling pin. Cut each rectangle lengthwise into 1-inch-wide strips, then crosswise into quarters. Place on ungreased cookie sheets. Reroll trimmings and cut.
3 Bake in hot oven (425°) 7 minutes, or until golden. Remove from cookie sheets to wire racks; cool completely. Store in a tightly covered container.

Butterscotch Chews

Children and grownups will make these bar cookies disappear in no time

Bake at 350° for 30 minutes.
Makes 16 squares

1 cup sifted all-purpose flour
1 teaspoon baking powder
¼ teaspoon salt
1 cup firmly packed light brown sugar
4 tablespoons (½ stick) butter or margarine, melted
1 egg, beaten
1 teaspoon vanilla
2 cups cornflakes

1 Sift flour, baking powder and salt into a large bowl. Stir in brown sugar, melted butter or margarine, egg and vanilla until well blended. Stir in 1½ cups of the cornflakes.
2 Spread in a greased baking pan, 8x8x2. Sprinkle remaining ½ cup cornflakes over top; press in firmly.

3 Bake in moderate oven (350°) 30 minutes, or until firm on top. Cool completely in pan on a wire rack. Cut in quarters lengthwise, then crosswise.

Walnut Wafers

Make the wafers any shape you like—the taste-treat is always good

Bake at 375° for 7 to 8 minutes.
Makes 6 dozen cookies

1 roll (11½ ounces) butterscotch-nut icebox-cookie dough
½ cup granulated sugar
1 cup halved or broken walnuts

1 Cut icebox-cookie dough into ½-inch-thick slices; halve each; shape into balls; roll in sugar; place 1 inch apart on greased cookie sheets; press walnut half in center of each.
2 Bake in moderate oven (375°) 7 to 8 minutes; cool cookies 1 minute, then remove and cool on wire racks.

Praline Crumb Squares

If you tire of squares, cut diagonally one way and then the other

Bake at 350° for 15 minutes.
Makes 3 dozen cookies

1 roll (11½ ounces) icebox-cookie dough, any flavor
¼ cup brown sugar, firmly packed

1 Cut off ¼ the roll and crumble into small bowl; mix in brown sugar.
2 Crumble remaining cookie dough into greased square pan, 8x8x2; heat in moderate oven (350°) 5 minutes (dough will melt and cover bottom); sprinkle with brown-sugar-dough mixture.
3 Bake 10 minutes longer, or until top is toasty-brown (do not overbake, as cookies should be chewy); cool in pan on wire rack; cut into small squares.

Caraway Cakes

The surprise time-saver here is packaged pancake mix

Bake at 350° for 6 to 7 minutes.
Makes 10 dozen small cookies

1½ cups pancake mix
½ cup sugar (for cookie dough)
1 tablespoon caraway seeds
1 egg
½ cup canned applesauce
2 tablespoons melted butter or margarine
¼ cup sugar (for topping)
1 teaspoon grated lemon peel

1 Combine pancake mix, ½ cup sugar and caraway seeds in medium-size bowl.
2 Beat egg slightly in small bowl; blend in applesauce and melted butter or margarine; stir into dry ingredients; mix well.
3 Drop by half-teaspoonfuls, 1 inch apart, on greased cookie sheets; sprinkle mixture of ¼ cup sugar and lemon peel on top.
4 Bake in moderate oven (350°) 6 to 7 minutes, or until edges are slightly browned; cool cookies 1 minute, then remove and cool completely on wire racks.

Peanut Drops

A perfect cookie to tuck into lunchboxes

Bake at 375° for 6 to 8 minutes.
Makes 7 dozen cookies

2 cups biscuit mix
1 cup brown sugar, firmly packed
1 teaspoon ground mace
¼ cup soft vegetable shortening
1 egg
⅓ cup milk
1 cup peanuts, chopped

1 Combine biscuit mix, sugar and mace in medium-size bowl; cut in shortening with pastry blender or 2 knives until mixture is consistency of coarse cornmeal.
2 Blend in egg and milk beaten together; sprinkle peanuts on dough and partly fold in. (If peanuts are very salty, rub between paper towels before chopping.)
3 Drop by teaspoonfuls, 1 inch apart, on greased cookie sheets.
4 Bake in moderate oven (375°) 6 to 8 minutes, or until golden-brown; remove and cool on wire racks.

MENUS

MENU

Quick Sauerbraten Steaks
Sweet-Sour Cabbage Medley
Mashed Potatoes
Farmhouse Cheese Relish
Nectarine Shortcakes

Work Plan

1 Start Nectarine Shortcakes: Slice and sugar fruit; chill. Slice pound cake; keep covered.
2 Prepare Farmhouse Cheese Relish; chill.
3 Set table.
4 Prepare Sweet-Sour Cabbage Medley.
5 While cabbage simmers, make first part of sauerbraten sauce; reserve.
6 Heat liquid ingredients for instant mashed potatoes, following label directions for 4 portions; make beverage.
7 Pan-broil steaks; finish potatoes.
8 Complete sauerbraten sauce.
9 At dessert time, assemble individual Nectarine Shortcakes.

Quick Sauerbraten Steaks

In just minutes, you can be ready to serve this jiffy version of a classic

Makes 4 servings

3 tablespoons butter or margarine
1 tablespoon all-purpose flour
½ teaspoon salt
½ teaspoon ground ginger
⅛ teaspoon pepper
⅛ teaspoon ground cloves
1 cup water
1 tablespoon light brown sugar
1 tablespoon mixed vegetable flakes
2 tablespoons red wine vinegar
4 individual steaks, 4 to 8 ounces each (chicken, king, cube, rib, minute, strip, etc.)

1 For first part of sauerbraten sauce, melt butter or margarine in a small saucepan; stir in flour, salt, ginger, pepper, and cloves. Cook, stirring constantly, just until bubbly. Stir in ½ cup of the water, brown sugar, vegetable flakes, and vinegar; continue cooking and stirring until sauce thickens and boils 1 minute. Cover; reserve for Step 3.
2 Pan-broil steaks to desired degree of done-

ness. (Chicken, steak, ½ inch thick, will cook to "medium" at 3 minutes on each side.) Remove from pan; keep warm.
3 Stir remaining ½ cup water into skillet, scraping to loosen brown glaze in pan. Add to reserved sauce; heat to boiling. Pour a little sauce over steaks; pass remainder in a heated sauce-dish.

Sweet-Sour Cabbage Medley

The contrasting flavors of tart apple and currant jelly combine to give cabbage a special tang

Makes 4 servings

1 small head of red cabbage (about 1 pound)
1 large tart apple (not pared)
2 tablespoons butter or margarine
1 medium-size onion, chopped (½ cup)
¼ cup red currant jelly
¼ cup water
2 tablespoons lemon juice
1 teaspoon salt

1 Shred cabbage. Halve, core, and dice apple.
2 Melt butter or margarine in large skillet; stir in cabbage, apple, onion, jelly, water, lemon juice, and salt until well blended; cover.
3 Heat to boiling. Simmer, stirring occasionally, about 25 minutes, or until liquid has almost evaporated and cabbage is tender.

Farmhouse Cheese Relish

Put this together in minutes and enjoy old-fashioned eating

Makes 4 servings

1 container (8 ounces) cream-style cottage cheese
1 medium-size dill pickle, diced and drained (¼ cup)
1 small carrot, shredded (¼ cup)
2 tablespoons dairy sour cream
2 tablespoons mayonnaise or salad dressing

1 Combine cottage cheese, dill pickle, and carrots in a medium-size bowl. Fold in sour cream and mayonnaise or salad dressing until well blended.
2 Chill until serving time. Sprinkle lightly with paprika, if you wish.

Nectarine Shortcakes

An easy-to-prepare quick dessert with the surprise of fresh fruit

Makes 4 servings

1 packaged pound cake (9 ounces)
4 cups sliced and sugared nectarines
1 container (4½ ounces) frozen whipped topping, thawed
Cinnamon-sugar

1 Cut pound cake into 8 slices; place 1 slice on each of 4 dessert plates; add half the nectarines, dividing evenly; top with remaining cake slices and remaining nectarines.
2 Spoon whipped topping over each portion. Sprinkle lightly with cinnamon-sugar. Serve at once.

MENU

Meat Ball Hotpot
Cucumbers Cairo
Bacon-Cheese Crescents
Pink Lemonade Cream

Work Plan

1 Prepare Meat Ball Hotpot; bake.
2 Meanwhile, make Pink Lemonade Cream; chill 15 minutes.
3 Prepare cucumbers for salad; add dressing; chill until serving time.
4 Prepare Bacon-Cheese Crescents; when Meat Ball Hotpot is done, remove from oven; raise temperature to 375°; bake crescents.
5 In the meantime, unmold Pink Lemonade Cream; garnish, if you wish; chill until serving time.
6 Make beverage; set table.
7 Place cucumber mixture in lettuce-lined bowl; add radishes; toss and serve.

Meat Ball Hotpot

Here's an easy-to-put-together hearty meal-in-a-dish

Bake at 350° for 45 minutes.
Makes 6 servings

1½ pounds meat-loaf mixture (ground beef, pork, and veal)

¾ cup seedless rye-bread crumbs
1 small onion, chopped (¼ cup)
1½ teaspoons salt
2 dashes Worcestershire sauce
1 egg
¾ cup buttermilk
2 packages (9 ounces each) frozen cut green beans
3 tablespoons vegetable oil
¼ cup sifted all-purpose flour
2½ cups water
1 envelope (2 to a package) onion-soup mix
½ teaspoon leaf thyme, crumbled
1 can (1 pound) small whole potatoes, drained
1 can or jar (4 ounces) pimientos, drained and diced

1 Combine meat-loaf mixture, bread crumbs, onion, salt, Worcestershire sauce, egg, and buttermilk in a large bowl; mix lightly until well blended. Shape into 36 balls.
2 Place the 2 packages green beans in a large bowl; cover with boiling water; reserve beans for Step 5.
3 Sauté meat balls until well browned, turning several times, in vegetable oil in a large skillet; remove with a slotted spoon to a deep 12-cup baking dish with cover.
4 Blend flour into drippings in skillet; cook, stirring constantly, until bubbly. Stir in the 2½ cups water, onion-soup mix, and thyme. Cook and stir, scraping to loosen brown glaze from pan, until gravy thickens and boils 1 minute.
5 Drain reserved green beans; add with potatoes to meat balls in baking dish; stir in gravy; place pimientos around edge; cover.
6 Bake in moderate oven (350°) 45 minutes, or until bubbly-hot.

Cucumbers Cairo

Dill and yogurt add sparkle to cucumbers and radishes

Makes 6 servings

2 large cucumbers
1 cup (8-ounce carton) plain yogurt
¼ cup bottled French dressing
1 teaspoon salt
1 teaspoon dillweed
1 small head iceberg lettuce
1 cup thinly sliced radishes

1 Pare cucumbers and slice thin; place in a medium-size bowl.

(continued)

2 Blend yogurt with French dressing, salt, and dillweed in a small bowl; pour over cucumbers; toss lightly to mix; chill.
3 At serving time, break lettuce into bite-size pieces; place in a salad bowl. Spoon cucumber mixture on top; add radishes; toss lightly to mix.

Bacon-Cheese Crescents

Dress up packaged rolls with cheese and sesame seeds

Bake at 375° for 15 minutes.
Makes 16 rolls

2 *packages (8 ounces each) refrigerated cres-cent dinner rolls*
1 *jar (5 ounces) pasteurized process cheese spread with bacon*
2 *tablespoons butter or margarine, melted*
2 *tablespoons sesame seeds*

1 Separate dough into 16 triangles; spread each with 1 teaspoon of the cheese spread. (Save remaining spread for snacks.) Roll up dough, following label directions.
2 Place rolls on ungreased cookie sheets; brush with melted butter or margarine; sprinkle with sesame seeds.
3 Bake in moderate oven (375°) 15 minutes, or until rolls are golden. Remove to wire rack. Serve warm.

Pink Lemonade Cream

Here's a taste treat for ice cream lovers

Makes 6 servings

1 *can (6 ounces) frozen concentrate for pink lemonade, thawed*
1 *quart vanilla ice cream, softened*
2 *envelopes unflavored gelatin*
4 *drops red food coloring*

1 Soften gelatin in the thawed lemonade concentrate in a small saucepan. Heat, stirring constantly, until gelatin dissolves; remove from heat.
2 Place softened ice cream in large bowl of electric mixer; beat until soft and creamy. Quickly add gelatin mixture and food coloring. Beat on medium speed 1 minute longer.
3 Immediately pour mixture into a 4-cup mold.

Place in refrigerator. Mold will "set" in 15 minutes.
4 Loosen around edge with a knife. Dip mold *very quickly* in and out of hot water. Cover with a serving plate; turn upside down; gently lift off mold. Garnish with whipped cream, if you wish. Serve immediately or chill until serving time.

MENU

Confetti-Frank Casserole
Snappy Corn Sticks
Taiwan Coleslaw
Frosty Cantaloupe Compotes

Work Plan

1 Prepare fruits for dessert; chill. Prepare dessert topping; chill.
2 Prepare Confetti-Frank Casserole; bake 20 minutes.
3 Meanwhile, shred vegetables for Taiwan Coleslaw; make slaw dressing; chill separately.
4 Top casserole with remaining frankfurters and cheese in pinwheel design.
5 Make beverage; set table.
6 Heat and season Snappy Corn Sticks; keep warm.
7 Toss Taiwan Coleslaw with dressing.
8 At dessert time, add topping to Frosty Cantaloupe Compotes.

Confetti-Frank Casserole

Franks and corn nestle in creamy rice for a satisfying supper

Bake at 375° for 40 minutes.
Makes 6 servings

1 *package (12 ounces) frozen rice pilaf in convenience cooking pouch*
1 *pound frankfurters*
1 *can (12 ounces) whole-kernel corn*
1 *can (10¾ ounces) condensed cream of celery soup*
4 *ounces process pasteurized cheese spread (from an 8-ounce package)*

1 Place rice pouch in a large bowl; fill with *very* hot water; let stand 5 minutes.
2 Cut 2 of the frankfurters in half lengthwise, then in half crosswise; reserve for topping. Cut remaining frankfurters into ½-inch slices; mix with corn and soup in a medium-size bowl. Cut

A happy combination of rice, corn, celery, cheese, and frankfurters result in snappy **Confetti Frank Casserole.**

cheese spread into 4 thin slices; cut each slice diagonally; reserve for topping.
3 Remove rice from pouch; break into small pieces; place in bottom of a 6-cup baking dish; top with frankfurter mixture, spreading evenly.
4 Bake in moderate oven (350°) 20 minutes. Place reserved frankfurters on top in pinwheel design; top each frankfurter with a section of cheese. Bake 20 minutes longer, or until cheese is melted and casserole is bubbly hot.

Snappy Corn Sticks

There's nothing difficult about these—they come from a package

Makes 6 servings

1 package (7 ounces) frozen corn sticks
2 tablespoons butter or margarine, melted
3 drops liquid red pepper seasoning

1 Heat corn sticks in toaster, following label directions.
2 Mix butter or margarine with liquid red pepper seasoning in a cup; brush over toasted corn sticks. Wrap sticks in foil; keep warm until ready to serve.

Taiwan Coleslaw

For slaw with a difference, start with Chinese cabbage

Makes 6 servings

6 cups shredded Chinese cabbage (from 1 small head)

3 medium-size carrots, pared and shredded
½ cup mayonnaise or salad dressing
1 tablespoon sugar
1 tablespoon lemon juice
½ teaspoon salt
⅛ teaspoon pepper

1 Combine cabbage and carrots in a large serving bowl. Cover; chill.
2 Mix mayonnaise or salad dressing, sugar, lemon juice, salt, and pepper in a small bowl; chill.
3 Just before serving, pour dressing over vegetable mixture; toss lightly to mix.

Frosty Cantaloupe Compotes

Chilled fruit topped with sour cream adds up to a perfect meal ender

Makes 6 servings

1 cup (8-ounce carton) dairy sour cream
⅓ firmly packed light brown sugar
¼ teaspoon ground cinnamon
1 medium-size ripe cantaloupe
1 pint fresh blueberries, rinsed and drained
½ pound seedless green grapes, rinsed, drained, and halved

1 Mix sour cream, brown sugar, and cinnamon in a small bowl. Cover; chill until ready to serve.
2 Cut cantaloupe into 6 wedges; remove seeds; place each wedge in a serving bowl. Divide blueberries and grapes evenly among bowls; cover with plastic wrap; chill until serving time.
3 To serve, spoon sour cream topping over fruit, dividing evenly.

MENU

Veal Piccata
Noodles Romanoff (from a mix)
Speedy Skillet Squash
Tomato-Artichoke Salad
Instant Zabaglione Berry Bowl

Work Plan

1 Assemble salad; add dressing; cover; chill.
2 Wash, drain, hull, and halve strawberries; cover; chill.
3 Cut vegetables for Speedy Skillet Squash.
4 Prepare Veal Piccata; reserve; keep warm.

(continued)

5 Cook Noodles Romanoff, following label directions.
6 Meanwhile, prepare Speedy Skillet Squash.
7 Make beverage; set table.
8 Prepare Instant Zabaglione; let stand 5 minutes.
9 Beat zabaglione; pour over strawberries; chill during dinner.
10 Drain salad; place in lettuce-lined bowl; serve.

Veal Piccata

This delicate veal and lemon dish takes only minutes to prepare

Makes 6 servings

1½ *pounds veal for scaloppine*
 ½ *cup unsifted all-purpose flour*
 2 *tablespoons butter or margarine*
 2 *tablespoons vegetable oil*
 1 *envelope instant chicken broth or 1 teaspoon granulated chicken-bouillon*
 1 *cup water*
 2 *lemons*
 Parsley sprigs

1 Dip veal in flour in a pie plate; tap off any excess.
2 Heat butter or margarine and oil until foaming in a large skillet. Brown veal, turning once, several pieces at a time; remove to a warm plate. (Add additional butter or margarine and oil to skillet during browning, if necessary.)
3 Stir chicken broth and water into skillet, scraping pan to loosen brown bits. Grate rind from one of the lemons, then squeeze juice. Stir rind and juice into sauce in pan. Return veal to skillet.
4 Simmer, covered, 15 minutes, or until veal is tender and sauce has thickened slightly.
5 Thinly slice remaining lemon; use as a garnish between veal slices; add parsley sprigs.

Speedy Skillet Squash

Oregano gives a surprise lift to zucchini

Makes 6 servings

 8 *small zucchini squash (weighing about 2 pounds)*
 4 *tablespoons butter or margarine (½ stick)*
 1 *medium-size onion, chopped (½ cup)*

 1 *teaspoon leaf oregano, crumbled*
 1 *teaspoon salt*
 ⅛ *teaspoon pepper*
 2 *tablespoons water*

1 Wash squash; drain; pat dry. (Do not pare.) Cut into thin slices.
2 Heat butter or margarine until foaming in a large skillet. Add onion; cook until soft but not brown.
3 Add squash; cook, stirring frequently, about 5 minutes. Stir in oregano, salt, pepper, and water. Cover; simmer 15 minutes, or until the squash is crisply tender.

Instant Zabaglione Berry Bowl

No one will believe it took so little time to whip up this creation

Makes 6 servings

 2 *pints strawberries*
1½ *cups cold milk*
 ½ *cup Marsala wine*
 1 *package (about 4 ounces) instant vanilla pudding*

1 Wash, drain, hull, and halve strawberries; place in a pretty glass serving bowl; chill.
2 Measure milk and Marsala in a 2-cup measure; pour into a medium-size bowl.
3 Add instant pudding; beat slowly with a rotary beater 2 minutes; let stand 5 minutes.
4 Beat zabaglione slowly with rotary beater for one minute; pour over strawberries. Chill during dinner.

Veal Piccata and **Speedy Skillet Squash** star in this fast-to-put-together menu.

Deep South Ham and Sweet Potatoes are the centerpiece in a quick-fix menu that will stamp you as a gourmet cook.

MENU

Appetizer Fruits
Deep South Ham and Sweet Potatoes
Green-and-Gold Vegetable Rings
Double-Cheese Salad Plates
Lemon Pudding Cups
Iced Tea

Work Plan

1 Heat oven.
2 Place butter or margarine for ham and sweet potatoes in baking pan; slide into oven to melt.
3 Prepare ham and sweet potatoes; place in oven.
4 Mix cupcake batter; bake.
5 Heat water for iced tea.
6 Add mint to fruit appetizer; chill.
7 Make lemon sauce for cupcakes; cool.
8 Cook corn and peas in separate saucepans.
9 Break salad greens; arrange with cheese strips on serving plates.
10 Make tea.
11 Remove cupcakes from oven; cool.
12 Drain vegetables; season.

13 Fill glasses with ice and tea.
14 Slice ham.
15 Drizzle salads with dressing.
16 Serve dinner.
17 Cut cupcakes and fill with sauce; serve.

Appetizer Fruits

Buy mixed fruit salad in the dairy case; add mint for a spring-fresh flavor

Makes 4 servings

2 cups mixed fruit salad (from a 2-pound jar)
Fresh mint

1 Place fruit salad in a bowl; crush several mint leaves and stir in. Chill to blend flavors.
2 Spoon into sherbet glasses; top each with a sprig of mint.

Deep South Ham and Sweet Potatoes

Two pantry-shelf stand-bys—canned ham and sweet potatoes—speed fixing and cooking

Bake at 375° for 25 minutes.
Makes 4 servings

4 tablespoons (½ stick) butter or margarine
⅓ cup honey
¼ teaspoon pumpkin-pie spice
2 tablespoons orange juice
1 one-pound canned ham
1 can (about 1 pound) sweet potatoes

1 Melt butter or margarine in a shallow baking pan while oven heats; remove and stir in honey, pumpkin-pie spice, and orange juice.
2 Place ham and sweet potatoes in pan; stud potatoes with whole cloves, if you wish; brush all with honey mixture.
3 Bake in moderate oven (375°), brushing several times with syrup in pan, 25 minutes, or until heated through and glazed.
4 Slice ham; arrange with sweet potatoes on serving plates. Garnish ham with spiced apple rings (from a jar) and parsley, and serve with prepared mustard, if you wish.

Green-and-Gold Vegetable Rings

Seasoned peas and whole-kernel corn make such colorful platemates

Makes 4 servings

1 package (10 ounces) frozen peas
1 package (10 ounces) frozen whole-kernel corn
2 tablespoons butter or margarine
½ teaspoon fines herbes

1 Cook frozen peas and corn in separate medium-size saucepans, following label directions; drain.
2 Season each with 1 tablespoon of the butter or margrine and ¼ teaspoon of the fines herbes.
3 Spoon peas into rings on serving plates; spoon corn into centers.

Double-Cheese Salad Plates

Strips of Swiss plus bottled blue-cheese dressing are the simple extras

Makes 4 servings

6 cups broken mixed salad greens

1 slice Swiss cheese (from an 8-ounce package), cut in thin strips
¼ cup bottled blue-cheese salad dressing

Divide salad greens among 4 serving plates; place cheese strips, crisscross fashion, on top. Just before serving, drizzle with blue-cheese dressing.

Lemon Pudding Cups

Cupcakes in a new guise—they have a luscious lemon filling you make in a wink

Bake at 375° for 20 minutes.
Makes 4 servings,
plus enough for at least one bonus treat

1 package yellow cupcake mix
2 eggs
½ cup milk
1 package lemon-flavor pudding and pie filling mix
Sugar
3 cups water
2 tablespoons butter or margarine
10X (confectioners' powdered) sugar

1 Prepare cupcake mix with 1 of the eggs and milk, following label directions; spoon into 12 greased large muffin-pan cups.
2 Bake in moderate oven (375°) 20 minutes, or until tops spring back when lightly pressed with fingertip.
3 Cool in pan on a wire rack 5 minutes; turn out onto rack.
4 While cupcakes bake, combine pudding and pie filling mix with sugar, following label directions, and remaining egg; stir in water. Cook, stirring constantly, until mixture thickens and comes to a full boil; remove from heat. Stir in butter or margarine until melted.
5 Cut a cone-shape piece from center of each of 4 cupcakes; place cupcakes on dessert plates; spoon ⅓ cup of the lemon sauce into hollows. Invert a cutout on top of each; dust with 10X sugar. Serve warm.
Note—Wrap remaining cupcakes and chill remaining sauce for another dessert or snacktime treat.

MENU

Egg Rolls with Mustard Sauce
(frozen-variety)
Oriental Beef Platter
Steamed Rice
Spiced Fruit Compote
Almond Cookies
Hot Tea

Work Plan

1 Tenderize beef, slice, and season.
2 Heat water for rice.
3 Heat frozen egg rolls in a frying pan, following label directions. (Buy the kind that are packaged with mustard sauce.)
4 Make mustard sauce for egg rolls, following label directions; let stand.
5 Arrange fruits for dessert in bowl; season; chill.
6 Cook rice.
7 Sauté beef strips.
8 Add broccoli to pan with beef.
9 Heat water for tea.
10 Make sauce for broccoli.
11 Brew tea.
12 Serve dinner.

Oriental Beef Platter

Strips of quick-cooking flank steak go with broccoli and rice for this meal-in-one

Makes 6 servings

1 flank steak (about 2 pounds)
Instant unseasoned meat tenderizer
2 tablespoons chopped crystallized ginger and syrup
2 tablespoons lemon juice
1 teaspoon seasoned salt
2 tablespoons peanut oil or vegetable oil
2 packages (10 ounces each) frozen chopped broccoli
1 can (3 or 4 ounces) sliced mushrooms
1 tablespoon cornstarch
2 tablespoons soy sauce
2 tablespoons water
4 cups hot cooked rice
¼ cup chopped pimiento·

1 Moisten steak and sprinkle with meat tenderizer, following label directions; cut diagonally into thin strips. Combine with crystallized ginger and syrup, lemon juice, and seasoned salt in a shallow dish; let stand 10 minutes to season. Lift strips from sauce; set dish aside.
2 Heat peanut oil or vegetable oil in a large frying pan; add beef strips and brown quickly; push to one side. Place frozen broccoli in pan; cover.
3 Steam 3 minutes; break up broccoli with a fork; pour sliced mushrooms and liquid over top. Steam 3 minutes longer, or until broccoli is crisply tender; push to one side.
4 Blend cornstarch, soy sauce, and water in a cup; stir into liquid in pan; cook, stirring constantly, until sauce thickens and boils 3 minutes.
5 Spoon beef strips and broccoli at ends of a large deep platter; spoon hot rice between. Garnish rice with pimiento; pour sauce in pan over broccoli; spoon any saved ginger sauce from dish over beef.

Spiced Fruit Compote

With three canned fruits, this colorful meal top-off is ready in a jiffy

Makes 6 servings

1 can (about 1 pound) cling peach halves
1 can or jar (about 1 pound) figs
1 can (about 11 ounces) mandarin-orange segments
¼ teaspoon ground cardamom
¼ cup flaked coconut

1 Drain syrup from peaches, figs, and mandarin-orange segments into a small bowl; arrange fruits in rings in a shallow glass bowl.
2 Stir cardamom into ½ cup of the syrup; pour over fruits; chill. (Save any remaining syrup for a breakfast beverage or to use in fruit gelatin.)
3 Just before serving, spoon coconut in a cone shape on top of fruits.

MENU

Mandarin Fruit Cup
Chinese Chicken with Rice
Sesame Snow Peas
Almond Cookies
Tea

Work Plan

1 Make appetizer fruit cup; place in freezer to chill quickly.
2 Slice chicken, celery, red pepper, green

(continued)

onions, mushrooms, and bamboo shoots, if needed, for main dish.

3 Toast sesame seeds for snow peas.

4 Measure water and salt for rice into a saucepan.

5 Sauté chicken.

6 Cook rice; keep hot.

7 Add vegetables plus seasonings to chicken and continue cooking.

8 Cook snow peas; keep hot.

9 Make sauce for chicken.

10 Make tea.

11 Serve dinner.

Mandarin Fruit Cup

Preparing this involves nothing more than opening two cans, but it's impressive

Makes 6 servings

2 cans (11 ounces each) mandarin-orange segments

1 can (about 1 pound, 5 ounces) pineapple tidbits

2 tablespoons chopped preserved ginger

2 tablespoons ginger syrup

2 tablespoons frozen concentrate for pineapple-orange juice

1 Drain syrups from orange segments and pineapple into a small bowl; save to add to punch. Combine fruits in a medium-size bowl. Stir in remaining ingredients. Chill.

2 Spoon into sherbet glasses. Garnish with slices of preserved ginger, if you wish.

Chinese Chicken with Rice

It takes a little time to get things ready but the cooking is easy and the eating superb.

Makes 6 servings

3 boneless chicken breasts (chicken cutlets), weighing about 1¾ pounds

½ pound mushrooms

1 can (5 ounces) bamboo shoots

3 green onions

1 small stalk celery

1 small sweet red pepper

OR: 1 can or jar (4 ounces) pimientos

4 tablespoons vegetable oil

¼ cup dry sherry

2 tablespoons soy sauce

2 tablespoons cornstarch

1 cup chicken broth (from an about-14-ounce can)

2 cups precooked rice (from a 14-ounce package)

Boiling water

Salt

1 Pull skin from chicken breasts; slice meat thin. Trim mushrooms and slice. Drain bamboo shoots and slice, if needed; trim green onions and celery; slice both thin. Halve red pepper, seed, and dice. (If using pimientos, drain and cut into strips.)

2 Sauté chicken quickly in vegetable oil in a large frying pan 3 minutes, or until chicken turns white.

3 Stir in mushrooms, bamboo shoots, green

If you've never been to the Orient, but always wanted to, settle for the moment for **Mandarin Fruit Cup** and **Chinese Chicken with Rice.** You'll be delighted with your away-from-home meal.

onions, celery, and red pepper; sauté 2 minutes. Stir in sherry and soy sauce; cover. Cook 2 minutes, or until vegetables are crisply tender.
4 Blend cornstarch into chicken broth until smooth in a small bowl; stir into frying pan. Cook, stirring constantly, until sauce thickens and boils for 3 minutes.
5 While chicken mixture cooks, prepare rice with boiling water and salt, following label directions. Spoon around edge on a large serving platter; spoon chicken mixture on top. Garnish with a half mushroom and serve with additional soy sauce, if you wish.

Sesame Snow Peas

Toasted sesame seeds add a special lift to snow peas in minutes

Makes 6 servings

2 tablespoons sesame seeds
2 packages (7 ounces each) snow peas
4 tablespoons (½ stick) butter or margarine
1 teaspoon lemon juice

1 Place sesame seeds in a small frying pan. Heat slowly, shaking pan constantly, until seeds are golden brown. Remove from heat and set aside for Step 3.
2 Cook snow peas, following label directions; drain.
3 Add butter or margarine, lemon juice, and sesame seeds to pan; heat slowly just until butter melts.

MENU

French Onion Soup
Butter-Broiled Halibut Steak
Savory Potato Puffs
(frozen variety)
Snowcap Tomatoes
Salad Asparagus
Frosted Pineapple Crescents
Hot Coffee

Work Plan

1 Heat broiler.
2 Cook frozen asparagus, following label directions.
3 Cut pineapple; place on serving plates; chill.
4 Melt 6 tablespoons (¾ stick) butter or marga-

rine for brushing on fish, tomatoes, and French bread.
5 Spread potato puffs in a shallow pan; sprinkle with seasoned salt. Heat in oven while fish broils.
6 Brush halibut steaks with melted butter or margarine; place on rack in broiler pan. Broil 5 minutes.
7 Drain asparagus; season; let stand.
8 Cut tomatoes and season.
9 Turn halibut; place tomatoes alongside on broiler rack. Continue broiling both.
10 Heat onion soup.
11 Slice French bread; toast; season with melted butter or margarine and cheese.
12 Mix topping for tomatoes.
13 Make coffee.
14 Cut lemon wedges for fish.
15 Serve dinner.
16 Scoop sherbet on pineapple and serve.

French Onion Soup

Slice of cheese-topped toast floats on each bowl for a Continental touch

Makes 4 servings

1 can (10½ ounces) condensed onion soup
  Water
4 thin slices French bread
1 tablespoon butter or margarine, melted
  Grated Parmesan cheese

1 Combine onion soup and water, following label directions, in a medium-size saucepan; heat to boiling.
2 While soup heats, toast bread; brush each slice with melted butter or margarine; sprinkle with cheese.
3 Ladle soup into cups or soup bowls; float a toast slice on each.

Butter-Broiled Halibut Steak

Fish goes from freezer to broiler to table in just 15 minutes

Makes 4 servings

2 packages (12 ounces each) frozen halibut steaks
3 tablespoons butter or margarine, melted
  Salt and pepper
  Paprika
1 lemon, cut in wedges

(continued)

Quick-fix recipes don't have to cut out the taste, as these recipes show: **Butter-Broiled Halibut Steak, Savory Potato Puffs, Salad Asparagus,** and **Snowcap Tomatoes.**

1 Place frozen halibut steaks on rack in broiler pan; brush with melted butter or margarine.
2 Broil, 4 to 6 inches from heat, 5 minutes; turn. Brush with remaining melted butter or margarine; sprinkle with salt, pepper, and paprika. Broil 8 minutes longer, or until fish flakes easily.
3 Place on serving plates; garnish each with a lemon wedge dipped in chopped parsley, if you wish.

Snowcap Tomatoes

A cool topping of blue-cheese cream contrasts so invitingly with buttery broiled tomatoes

Makes 4 servings

2 large firm ripe tomatoes
2 tablespoons butter or margarine, melted
½ teaspoon sugar
½ teaspoon salt
  Dash of pepper
½ cup dairy sour cream
2 tablespoons crumbled blue cheese

1 Halve tomatoes crosswise; brush cut sides with melted butter or margarine; sprinkle with sugar, salt, and pepper. Place beside fish on rack in broiler pan.
2 Broil, 4 to 6 inches from heat, 8 minutes, or until bubbly on top.
3 While tomatoes heat, blend sour cream and blue cheese in a cup. Spoon over tomatoes just before serving.

Salad Asparagus

Seasoned with French dressing and served slightly warm, it doubles as salad and a second vegetable

Makes 4 servings

1 package (10 ounces) frozen asparagus
  spears
¼ cup bottled French dressing
4 romaine leaves

1 Cook asparagus, following label directions; drain. Drizzle with French dressing. Let stand at room temperature until serving time to season.
2 Place a romaine leaf on each serving plate; arrange asparagus spears on top. Garnish each with a strip of pimiento tied into a knot, if you wish.

Frosted Pineapple Crescents

Sherbet balls crown wedges of juicy golden pineapple for this simple fancy

Makes 4 servings

1 small ripe pineapple
1 pint lemon sherbet

1 Cut pineapple in quarters lengthwise, right through leafy crown. Cut core from each quarter.

2 Loosen fruit from rind in one piece by cutting close to round shell base. (A grapefruit knife and a sawing motion speed the job.) Halve fruit lengthwise, then cut crosswise into bite-size pieces; chill until serving time.
3 When ready to serve, place each quarter on a serving plate; top with a scoop of lemon sherbet. .

MENU

Quick Veal Goulash
Poppy-Seed Noodles
Continental Salad Toss
Hard Rolls
Raspberry Cream Stacks
Hot Coffee

Work Plan

1 Heat kettle of water for noodles.
2 Place beets for salad in a serving bowl. Slice endive; combine with beets and season; chill.
3 Sauté veal for goulash.
4 Cook noodles.
5 Fix sauce for goulash.
6 Make coffee.
7 Drain noodles; season.
8 Place veal in sauce; heat.
9 Set out jam, almonds, cocoa mix, and serving plates for dessert.
10 Serve dinner.
11 Toast waffles; put dessert together; serve.

Quick Veal Goulash

Fast-cooking veal in a spicy tomato sauce tops buttery noodles for this hearty

Makes 4 servings

4 cube veal steaks
   OR: 1 pound veal for scaloppine
4 tablespoons (½ stick) butter or margarine
2 large onions, chopped (2 cups)
2 tablespoons all-purpose flour
1 tablespoon paprika
1 teaspoon salt
1 teaspoon marjoram

1 can (about 1 pound) stewed tomatoes
½ cup water
POPPY-SEED NOODLES *(recipe follows)*

1 Sauté veal in 2 tablespoons of the butter or margarine in a large frying pan 3 minutes; turn. Brown other side; remove from pan; keep warm.
2 Stir onions into pan with remaining 2 tablespoons butter or margarine; cover. Cook 5 minutes, or until onions are tender.
3 Sprinkle flour, paprika, salt, and marjoram over top, then blend in; stir in tomatoes and water. Cook, stirring constantly, until sauce thickens and boils 1 minute.
4 Place veal in sauce; heat slowly just until bubbly-hot.
5 Spoon POPPY-SEED NOODLES into a large shallow serving bowl; spoon veal and sauce over top.

Poppy-Seed Noodles

Just a sprinkle of these tiny seeds is enough for a dressy touch

Makes 4 servings

1 package (8 ounces) fine noodles
1 tablespoon butter or margarine
1 tablespoon poppy seeds

1 Cook noodles in a kettle of rapidly boiling salted water, following label directions; drain; return to kettle.
2 Add butter or margarine and poppy seeds; toss lightly to mix.

Continental Salad Toss

With lots of beets, it can take the place of vegetable and salad

Makes 4 servings

1 jar (1 pound) sliced pickled beets
2 medium-size stalks Belgian endive, trimmed
2 tablespoons bottled oil-and-vinegar dressing
2 tablespoons chopped parsley

1 Drain beets; pile in the center of a shallow serving bowl.
2 Cut endive crosswise into thin slices; place in a ring around beets; drizzle with oil-and-vinegar dressing. Sprinkle beets with parsley.
3 Just before serving, toss lightly to mix.

Raspberry Cream Stacks

Your speedy helpers: Frozen waffles, ice cream, jam, and ready-whipped cream

Makes 4 servings

4 frozen waffles
4 tablespoons red raspberry jam
1 pint vanilla ice cream
4 teaspoons toasted slivered almonds (from a 5-ounce can)
Whipped cream from a pressurized can
1 teaspoon instant cocoa mix

1 Toast frozen waffles, following label directions; spread each with 1 tablespoon of the jam; place on serving plates.
2 Top each with a generous scoop of ice cream, almonds, and a dollop of whipped cream; sprinkle cocoa mix over cream.

MENU

Shrimp Appetizer-Salad
Veal Napoli
Peas in Potato Nest
Corn on the Cob   Paprika Butter
Parmesan Rolls
Ruby Rice Crown

Shrimp Appetizer-Salad

Ready-to-go shrimp cocktails from your dairy case are the key to this dinner starter that doubles as the salad course.

Makes 4 servings

4 glasses (4 ounces each) ready-to-serve refrigerated shrimp cocktail
3 cups finely shredded lettuce
¼ cup mayonnaise or salad dressing
1 tablespoon sweet-pickle relish

1 Drain sauce from shrimp cocktails into a small bowl. (Tip to speed the job: Just empty the shrimps into a strainer set over a bowl.)
2 Place lettuce in 4 serving dishes or on salad plates; spoon shrimps on top.
3 Blend mayonnaise or salad dressing and pickle relish into ¼ cup of the cocktail sauce

in a 1-cup measure; serve separately to spoon over shrimps. (Save any remaining cocktail sauce to season stew or to use as a sandwich spread for another day.)

Veal Napoli

Quick-cooking scaloppine meat and ready-seasoned tomatoes for the sauce go in and out of the frying pan in a hurry.

Makes 4 servings

1 pound veal for scaloppine
4 tablespoons (½ stick) butter or margarine
Salt and pepper
1 can (3 or 4 ounces) sliced mushrooms
1 can (about 8 ounces) stewed tomatoes

1 Brown veal quickly, a few pieces at a time, in butter or margarine in a large frying pan; sprinkle lightly with salt and pepper; remove and keep warm while making sauce.
2 Stir mushrooms and liquid and tomatoes into drippings in frying pan; heat to boiling, scraping browned bits from bottom of pan, then cook 5 minutes, or until sauce thickens slightly.
3 Place veal in sauce; heat slowly 1 minute, or just until hot. Spoon onto serving plates.

Peas in Potato Nests

For speed, call on instant mashed potatoes and use chicken soup as the liquid.

Makes 4 servings

1 package (10 ounces) frozen green peas and celery
1 can (10½ ounces) condensed cream of chicken soup
1 soup can of water
1 envelope (2 to a package) instant mashed potatoes

1 Cook peas and celery, following label directions; keep hot.
2 Mix soup and water in a medium-size saucepan; heat, stirring constantly, to boiling. Add instant potatoes; whip with a fork or wooden spoon until smooth.
3 Spoon onto serving plates; hollow center of each mound with a spoon to make a nest; spoon peas into hollows.

Parmesan Rolls

A smidgen of zesty cheese broils atop Parker House rolls for these bake-day quickies

Makes 4 servings

8 ready-baked Parker House rolls
1 tablespoon butter or margarine, melted
4 teaspoons grated Parmesan cheese

1 Place rolls in a shallow pan; brush with melted butter or margarine; sprinkle with cheese.
2 Broil, 4 to 6 inches from heat, 1 to 2 minutes, or until cheese is golden. Serve hot.

Ruby Rice Crown

Sparkly currant sauce tops cooked apples in the creamiest rice mold. Make well ahead of time

Makes 6 servings

1 cup uncooked regular rice
3 cups milk
¼ teaspoon salt
¾ cup sugar
1 teaspoon vanilla
2 egg yolks, slightly beaten
2 tablespoons butter or margarine
1 cup water
2 tablespoons lemon juice
⅛ teaspoon ground allspice
3 medium-size apples, pared, halved, and cored
1 jar (10 ounces) red currant jelly

1 Cook rice in a large amount of boiling water 5 minutes in a medium-size saucepan; drain.
2 Scald milk in the top of a double boiler over simmering water; stir in salt and drained rice. Cook, covered, over simmering water, 1 hour, or until rice is very soft. Stir in ¼ cup of the sugar, vanilla, egg yolks, and butter or margarine; spoon into a fancy 4-cup ring or tube mold. Chill at least 2 hours, or until serving time.
3 Combine water, remaining ½ cup sugar, lemon juice, and allspice in a medium-size saucepan; heat to boiling; add apples; cover. Simmer very slowly, turning apples once, 15 minutes, or until tender but still firm enough to hold their shape; lift out with a slotted spoon and drain on paper toweling. Chill.
4 Blend ¼ cup of the apple syrup into currant jelly in a small saucepan; heat, stirring constantly, until jelly melts.
5 When ready to serve, loosen rice mold around edge with a knife. Invert onto a serving plate; shake gently, if needed, to loosen; lift off mold carefully.
6 Leave one half apple whole and cut each of remaining into quarters; place part in center of mold and arrange remaining, spoke fashion, around edge of top; place saved half in center. Spoon part of the currant sauce over apples, then serve remaining separately.

A spread like this would spark up any buffet, yet every dish comes from a package.

Pantry Shelf Cooking

Putting all the ingredients together for a fast meal can tax the ingenuity of the most seasoned cook. But with the staples kept on the shelf, ingenuity becomes instant availability. From the cake mix to shake 'n bake, there are a host of convenience foods and mixes that can make light work out of any quick-fix meal time.

SOUPS

Mushroom Bisque

Make this in no time for a special occasion

Makes 4 to 6 servings

1 envelope (2 to a package) mushroom soup mix
1 tablespoon grated onion
2 cups water
Dash of ground allspice
1½ cups light cream or table cream
1 teaspoon lemon juice

1 Prepare soup mix with onion and water, following label directions; cool.
2 Beat in remaining ingredients. Chill.
3 Pour into chilled cups or mugs. Garnish with chopped parsley, if you wish.

Clam Stew

This version of a New England favorite is a meal in itself

Makes 6 servings

1 small onion, minced (¼ cup)
¼ cup minced celery
2 tablespoons butter or margarine
1 can (about 8 ounces) minced clams
3 cups milk
1 teaspoon Worcestershire sauce
Few drops liquid red pepper seasoning
½ cup dry instant mashed potatoes
1 tablespoon chopped parsley

1 Sauté onion and celery in butter or margarine until soft in a large saucepan.

2 Stir in clams and liquid, milk, Worcestershire sauce and liquid red pepper seasoning. Heat just to boiling; remove from heat.
3 Stir in instant potatoes and parsley until mixture thickens slightly.
4 Ladle into soup bowls or cups. Serve with your favorite crackers.

Pea Soup Chowder

Canned soup, plus chick peas and seasonings, makes this hearty lunch soup

Makes 4 to 6 servings

1 cup sliced celery
1½ cups water
1 can (11¼ ounces) condensed green-pea soup
1 can (about 1 pound) chick peas
¼ cup chili sauce
1 tablespoon grated onion
¼ teaspoon mixed Italian herbs
1 beef-bouillon cube

1 Simmer celery in water 10 minutes, or just until crisply tender, in a medium-size saucepan.
2 Stir in remaining ingredients, crushing bouillon cube with spoon. Heat to boiling, then simmer 5 minutes.
3 Ladle into heated soup bowls or cups.

Country Chicken Chowder

Canned soup, canned corn, canned milk—what could be easier?

Makes 6 servings

1 medium-size onion, chopped (½ cup)
2 tablespoons butter or margarine
2 cans (10¾ ounces each) condensed chicken-noodle soup
1 soup can water
1 can (about 1 pound) cream-style corn
1 small can evaporated milk (⅔ cup)
¼ teaspoon pepper
2 tablespoons chopped parsley

1 Sauté onion in butter or margarine just until soft in medium-size saucepan.

(continued)

When you need something warm and fast, serve up a canned-food quickie soup and a vegetable salad.

2 Stir in remaining ingredients, except parsley. Heat just to boiling.
3 Pour into heated soup bowls or mugs; sprinkle with parsley.

Frosty Tomato Cream

Smooth and cold and just the starter for a meal on a hot day

Makes 6 servings

1 can (10¾ ounces) condensed chicken broth
  well chilled
1 can (10¾ ounces) condensed tomato soup,
  well chilled
1 cup light cream or table cream
1 small cucumber, pared and cut up
1 small onion, peeled and cut up
8 sprigs of parsley
  Thin cucumber slices
  Fresh dill sprigs

1 Skim any fat from chicken broth; combine soups in an electric-blender container. Add light cream or table cream; the cut-up cucumber, the onion and parsley. Cover and beat until almost smooth.

2 Chill several hours or until frosty-cold. Pour into a tureen or small cups or bowls; float thin cucumber slices and fresh dill sprigs on top.

Finnish Fruit "Soup"

Try this unusual Scandinavian soup

Makes 8 servings

1 package (3 ounces) lemon-flavor gelatin
1 cup boiling water
1 cup cold water
1 can (1 pound, 13 ounces) fruit cocktail
1 jar (16 ounces) citrus fruit salad (from dairy
  case)
¼ cup lemon juice

1 Dissolve gelatin in boiling water in a large bowl; stir in cold water, fruit cocktail and syrup, fruit salad and juice and lemon juice. Chill several hours, or until very cold.
2 When ready to serve, ladle into a glass serving bowl or individual serving dishes. Garnish with mint, if you wish. Serve as an appetizer.

Note—If soup chills overnight, gelatin will set softly.

Confetti Chowder

There's much more to this exquisite dish than a mere sprinkling

Makes 8 servings

1 package (12 ounces) smoked sausage links
2 tablespoons butter or margarine
1 large onion, chopped (1 cup)
2 packages (10 ounces each) frozen mixed vegetables
1 cup water
6 cups reconstituted instant nonfat dry milk
1 tablespoon prepared mustard
2 teaspoons salt
¼ teaspoon pepper
1 cup dry instant mashed potatoes

1 Slice sausages 1 inch thick; brown in butter or margarine in a heavy kettle; remove and set aside. Stir onion into drippings; sauté until soft.
2 Stir in mixed vegetables and water; cook, following label directions. Stir in milk, mustard, salt, pepper and sausages. Heat slowly, stirring several times, to boiling.
3 Slowly stir in dry potatoes until mixture thickens slightly. Ladle into heated soup bowls; serve with chowder crackers.

VEGETABLES

Casserole Creamed Vegetables

Even those who shy away from vegetables will go for this dish

Bake at 375° for 1 hour.
Makes 8 servings

2 packages (9 ounces each) frozen French fried potatoes
Boiling water
2 packages (9 ounces each) frozen cut green beans
1 can (3½ ounces) French fried onions
1 can (10¾ ounces) condensed cream of mushroom soup
⅔ cup milk
2 tablespoons chopped pimientos
½ teaspoon salt
⅛ teaspoon pepper

1 Place frozen potatoes in a strainer; pour boiling water over top; drain well. Pile in center of a greased deep 12-cup baking dish.
2 Place frozen beans in strainer; pour boiling water over top; drain well. Mix with half of the onions in a medium-size bowl; spoon around edge in baking dish.
3 Blend mushroom soup with milk, pimientos, salt and pepper in a small bowl; pour over vegetable mixture; cover.
4 Bake in moderate oven (375°) 55 minutes; uncover. Sprinkle remaining onions over top. Bake 5 minutes longer, or until vegetables are tender and onions are hot.

Duchess Vegetables

Here's an unusual and attractive way to serve vegetables

Bake at 375° for 40 minutes.
Makes 6 servings

3 cups prepared instant mashed potatoes
1 can (1 pound) sliced carrots, drained
2 cans (1 pound each) cut green beans, drained
Salt
Pepper
½ teaspoon leaf marjoram, crumbled
3 tablespoons butter or margarine

1 Spoon mashed potatoes into a 9-inch pie plate, building up edge to form a shell.
2 Place carrots in a row across middle in shell; spoon green beans on each side; sprinkle with salt, pepper and marjoram. Dot with butter or margarine. Cover loosely with foil.
3 Bake in moderate oven (375°) 40 minutes, or until vegetables are hot.

Savory Oven Vegetables

This is a sure-fire, no-fuss quickie

Bake at 425° for 30 minutes.
Makes 4 servings

1 package (10 ounces) frozen mixed vegetables
2 tablespoons butter or margarine
2 tablespoons water
½ teaspoon salt
½ teaspoon dillweed

(continued)

1 Combine frozen mixed vegetables, butter or margarine, water, salt, and dillweed in a 4-cup baking dish; cover.
2 Bake in hot oven (425°) 30 minutes, or until tender, stirring once to blend seasonings.

Creole Succotash

The beans blend deliciously with golden corn and ready-seasoned stewed tomatoes

Makes 6 servings

1 package (10 ounces) frozen baby lima beans
1 package (10 ounces) frozen whole-kernel corn
1 can (about 1 pound) stewed tomatoes
3 tablespoons butter or margarine

1 Cook lima beans, following label directions; when almost tender, add corn; heat to boiling; simmer 2 minutes. (If needed, add 1 or 2 table-spoons water to finish cooking, but when done, water should be absorbed.)
2 Stir in tomatoes; heat just until steaming hot; spoon succotash into serving dishes and top each with a pat of butter or margarine.

Green Bean Medley

You'll sing the praises of this easy-to-make green bean and onion combination

Makes 4 servings

1 package (9 ounces) frozen Italian green beans
Water
Salt
1 can (8 ounces) small boiled onions, drained
¼ cup chopped pimiento
2 tablespoons chopped parsley
1 tablespoon butter or margarine
½ teaspoon salt
⅛ teaspoon pepper
⅛ teaspoon garlic powder

1 Cook green beans with water and salt, follow-ing label directions, in a medium-size saucepan. Drain.
2 Combine green beans with pimiento, parsley, butter or margarine, salt, pepper and garlic powder in same saucepan. Heat until bubbly-hot.

Onions Mornay

For serving, spoon the creamy sauce over the toasty bread—what good eating!

Bake at 350° for 30 minutes.
Makes 6 servings

4 tablespoons (½ stick) butter or margarine
2 large sweet onions, coarsely chopped (2 cups)
2 cloves garlic, minced
1 can (10¾ ounces) condensed cream of celery soup
1 cup milk
¼ teaspoon seasoned pepper
1 can (1 pound) cut green beans, drained
2 packages (8 ounces each) sliced process Swiss cheese
12 half-inch-thick slices French bread

1 Melt butter or margarine in a large frying pan; stir in onions and garlic; cover. Cook 15 min-utes; stir in soup, milk and pepper; heat, stirring several times, until bubbly.
2 Make two layers each of beans, cheese slices and sauce in a buttered 8-cup baking dish; arrange bread slices, overlapping, on top.
3 Bake in moderate oven (350°) 30 minutes, or until bubbly-hot.

Rice Verde

An attractive dish, surround it with meat of your choosing

Makes 4 servings

1 package (9 ounces) frozen creamed spinach (in pouch)
Packaged precooked rice
Water
Salt
Butter or margarine
Dash of nutmeg

1 Heat spinach, as label directs.
2 Prepare rice with water, salt and butter or margarine, following label directions to make 3 cups.
3 Combine spinach, rice and nutmeg in a large bowl; mixing well. Spoon into a well-buttered 4-cup ring mold. Let stand 5 minutes in a warm place.
4 To unmold, cover ring mold with a heated serving platter; turn both over together; shake gently; lift off mold.

A melange of meats and vegetables go together for outdoor fix-ups.

Milano Potato Mold

Instant mashed potatoes are flavored with Parmesan cheese and layered and baked with provolone

Bake at 350° for 1 hour.
Makes 6 to 8 servings

2 tablespoons fine dry bread crumbs
Instant mashed potatoes
Water
Butter or margarine
Salt
2 eggs
¼ cup grated Parmesan cheese
2 tablespoons chopped parsley
⅛ teaspoon pepper
4 slices provolone cheese (from an 8-ounce package)

1 Butter a 6-cup ovenproof bowl; coat lightly with bread crumbs.
2 Prepare enough instant mashed potatoes with water, butter or margarine and salt (*omit milk*), following label directions, to make 3 cups. Beat in eggs, 1 at a time; stir in Parmesan cheese, parsley and pepper.
3 Spoon one third into prepared bowl; top with 2 slices of the provolone cheese. Repeat layers; spoon remaining potato mixture on top.
4 Bake in moderate oven (350°) 1 hour, or until golden and potatoes start to pull away from side of bowl. Cool in bowl on a wire rack 10 minutes. Loosen mold around edge with a knife; tip and shake bowl gently to loosen mold from bottom; invert onto a heated serving plate; lift off bowl. Serve hot.

Potatoes Delmonico

It's amazing how fast you can make this classic potato recipe with new products

Bake at 350° about 45 minutes.
Makes 6 to 8 servings

9 cups water
1 teaspoon salt
1 package (8 ounces) dehydrated sliced potatoes (4½ cups)
1 can (10½ ounces) chicken gravy
1 tablespoon grated onion
1 teaspoon dry mustard
1 teaspoon paprika
¼ teaspoon pepper
1¼ cups milk

2 packages (4 ounces each) shredded Cheddar cheese (2 cups)
2 pimientos, diced

1 Heat water to boiling in large saucepan; add salt and potatoes; cover; lower heat; cook 20 minutes.
2 While potatoes cook, combine chicken gravy, onion, mustard, paprika and pepper in 4-cup measure; gradually stir in milk.
3 Drain potatoes; place in baking dish, 13x9x2 sprinkle with cheese and pimientos; toss to mix; pour gravy mixture over; cover with foil.
4 Bake in moderate oven (350°) 45 minutes, or until bubbly-hot in the middle.

Parisian Potato Puff

Distinctive differences for the instant variety: Gruyère, onion, green pepper

Bake at 375° for 20 minutes.
Makes 6 servings

2 tablespoons chopped green pepper
2 tablespoons chopped green onion
1 tablespoon bacon drippings
4 cups prepared instant mashed potatoes
1 package (6 ounces) process Gruyère cheese, cut in small cubes
¼ cup bacon-flavor bits

1 Sauté green pepper and onion in bacon drippings until soft in a small frying pan; beat into mashed potatoes. Fold in three fourths of the cheese.
2 Spoon mixture into a 4-cup baking dish; sprinkle remaining cheese over top.
3 Bake in moderate oven (375°) 20 minutes, or until cheese melts and potatoes are lightly golden. Sprinkle bacon bits over top.

Skillet Potato Medley

For a change, brown frozen French fries, add seasoned tomatoes, and simmer

Makes 6 to 8 servings

1 large onion, chopped (1 cup)
1 cup chopped celery
3 tablespoons vegetable oil

1 bag (2 pounds) frozen French fried potatoes
2 teaspoons salt
¼ teaspoon pepper
1 can (about 1 pound) stewed tomatoes
1 tablespoon chopped parsley

1 Sauté onion and celery in vegetable oil until soft in a large frying pan. Stir in frozen potatoes; sprinkle salt and pepper over top. Cook slowly, stirring several times, until potatoes are golden.
2 Pour tomatoes and juice over potato mixture; stir lightly; cover. Heat slowly, stirring once or twice, until almost all liquid is absorbed. Spoon into a heated serving bowl; sprinkle with chopped parsley. Serve with broiled hamburger patties or steak.

MAIN DISHES

Beefeater's Platter

Flavorful chuck and the convenient canned sandwich make a satisfying stick-to-the-ribs dinner

Makes 6 to 8 servings

1 arm-bone beef chuck roast, weighing about 4 pounds
3 medium-size onions, peeled and sliced thin
1 can (15½ ounces) sandwich sauce
1 cup water
1 package (8 ounces) regular noodles
¼ cup chopped parsley

1 Trim fat from roast. Sauté enough of the trimmings in a heavy kettle or Dutch oven to make about 2 tablespoonfuls drippings; remove and discard.
2 Brown roast slowly in drippings; drain off fat. Stir in onions, sandwich sauce and water. Heat to boiling; cover. Simmer, turning meat several times, 2½ hours, or until tender. Place on a deep serving platter; keep warm.
3 While roast simmers, cook noodles, following label directions; drain. Spoon around roast on platter; sprinkle parsley over noodles.
4 Skim any fat from sauce; reheat to boiling. Spoon part over roast; serve remainder separately. Carve roast into serving-size slices.

Steak Piquant

Man-size chunks of beef bake with noodles, limas and tomatoes in this colorful entrée

Summer *30 min*
+Bake at 350° for 30 minutes.
60 min
Makes 6 servings

2 pounds lean round steak or beef chuck, cut into 1-inch cubes
2 tablespoons vegetable oil
½ cup water
2 beef-bouillon cubes
1½ teaspoons salt
½ teaspoon ground cardamom
¼ teaspoon pepper
1 tablespoon lemon juice
1 package (8 ounces) noodles
1 package (10 ounces) frozen baby lima beans
3 medium-size tomatoes, cut into wedges
1 teaspoon sugar
1 tablespoon finely chopped parsley

1 Brown beef cubes in vegetable oil in large frying pan. Stir in water, bouillon cubes, salt, cardamom, pepper and lemon juice. Cover; simmer 20 to 30 minutes, or until meat is tender.
2 Cook noodles, following label directions; drain; place in greased 12-cup baking dish.
3 Cook lima beans, following label directions; drain; spoon over noodles to make a ring around edge of baking dish.
4 Spoon meat in middle, then pour juices over all. Arrange tomato wedges, overlapping, on top of lima beans; sprinkle with sugar and salt and pepper, if desired; cover.
5 Bake in moderate oven (350°) 30 minutes to blend flavors. Sprinkle parsley over top just before serving.

Red-Flannel Hash

Everything is on your kitchen shelf to make this old-fashioned favorite

Makes 4 generous servings

1 can (1 pound) julienne beets
2 cans (1 pound each) corned-beef hash
1 tablespoon instant minced onion

1 Drain beets, then pat dry between sheets of paper toweling.
2 Break up corned-beef hash with a fork in a

(continued)

large bowl; mix in beets and onion. Shape into 8 thick patties.

3 Sauté slowly, turning only once, until crusty-brown in a large frying pan. (No need to add any fat.) Serve hot with catsup or prepared mustard, if you wish.

Cubed-Beef Stroganoff

This gourmet dish can be ready in minutes with leftover roast beef

Makes 6 servings

1 medium-size onion, chopped (½ cup)
2 tablespoons vegetable oil
3 cups cubed cooked beef
1 can (10¾ ounces) condensed tomato soup
1 can (3 or 4 ounces) chopped mushrooms
1 teaspoon sugar
1 cup dairy sour cream

1 Sauté onion in vegetable oil in large frying pan; add beef and brown lightly.

2 Stir in tomato soup, mushrooms and liquid and sugar; cover; simmer 20 minutes to blend flavors.

3 Stir in sour cream; heat just to boiling (don't let sauce boil, as sour cream may curdle). Serve over buttered hot noodles.

'70s Pizza

Packaged dinner rolls and meatloaf mixture make this a hearty family meal

Bake at 375° for 20 minutes.
Makes 4 servings

1 pound meat loaf mixture
1 tablespoon vegetable oil
1 envelope (1½ ounces) spaghetti sauce mix
1 can (8 ounces) tomato sauce
1 cup water
1 package (8 ounces) refrigerated butterflake dinner rolls
1 cup ricotta cheese
4 ounces mozzarella cheese, shredded (1 cup)
1 tablespoon grated Parmesan cheese

1 Brown meat loaf mixture in oil in a medium-size skillet until no pink remains (about 10 minutes); break into small pieces with a fork; sprinkle with spaghetti sauce mix; stir in tomato sauce, then water. Bring to boiling; reduce heat;

simmer, stirring often, 20 minutes, or until very thick.

2 Remove dinner rolls from package (12 rolls in package); separate each roll to make 24 thinner rolls; place 12 in a layer on bottom of a 9-inch pie plate; press edges together to cover bottom; spoon ½ cup ricotta evenly over roll layer; top with half the cooked meat mixture; sprinkle with ½ cup mozzarella; repeat layers of ricotta, meat and mozzarella; top with remaining rolls.

3 Bake in moderate oven (375°) 15 minutes; sprinkle with Parmesan cheese; bake 5 minutes longer, or until rolls are golden brown. Cut into wedges to serve.

Viennese Veal

From stove to table in just minutes with the help of canned soup

Makes 6 servings

1½ pounds cubed veal steaks
2 tablespoons vegetable oil
1 can (10½ ounces) mushroom gravy
½ cup water
1 cup dairy sour cream
¼ cup chopped parsley

1 Cut veal into serving-size pieces; sauté in vegetable oil in large frying pan over medium heat 5 minutes on each side, or until tender; remove veal to a heated platter; keep hot while you make the gravy.

2 Pour all excess fat from pan; stir in mushroom gravy and water; heat to boiling, stirring constantly; simmer 2 to 3 minutes.

3 Remove from heat; stir in sour cream and parsley until well blended; pour around meat; serve at once, as sour cream may curdle if reheated.

Onion-Sausage Pie

No one will believe it took so little time to make this spectacular dish

Bake at 375° for 40 minutes.
Makes 6 servings

2 frozen ready-to-bake 9-inch piecrusts
1 can (12 or 16 ounces) whole-kernel corn
1 can (about 1 pound) boiled onions with cream-sauce mix

A parade of quick-fix beauties, ranging from skin- crackling chicken to roasted marshmallows.

1 can (1 pound) white potatoes, drained and diced
1 package (8 ounces) heat-and-serve sausages, sliced
2 tablespoons butter or margarine
½ teaspoon salt
⅛ teaspoon pepper
2 teaspoons parsley flakes
3 hard-cooked eggs, shelled and diced
1 egg, beaten

1 Thaw both piecrusts, following label directions.
2 Drain liquid from corn into a 1-cup measure; drain liquid from onions; add enough onion liquid to corn liquid to make ¾ cup.
3 Sauté potatoes and sausages in butter or margarine until lightly browned in a large frying pan; stir in salt and pepper. Spoon mixture into a large bowl.
4 Stir the ¾ cup liquid into drippings in frying pan; add sauce mix from onions. Cook, stirring constantly, until sauce thickens and boils 1 minute. Stir into meat mixture with corn, onions, parsley flakes and hard-cooked eggs. Spoon into a shallow 6-cup baking dish.
5 Roll out 1 of the piecrusts on a pastry cloth or board to a rectangle, 12x10; working lengthwise, cut into 6 strips ¾ inch wide and 6 strips ¼ inch wide with a pastry wheel or knife. Brush wide strips lightly with part of the beaten egg; press a narrow strip on top of each. Weave strips over filling in dish to make a crisscross top; trim any overhang flush with rim of dish.
6 Repeat rolling, cutting, brushing and stacking
(continued)

There's a lot of quick-heated goodness in **Sausage Pizza:** salami, link sausages, and pepperoni.

with remaining piecrust. Brush ends of strips over filling with beaten egg; place remaining strips around rim of dish, overlapping slightly, to make a neat edge.

7 Bake in moderate oven (375°) 15 minutes; brush strips with remaining beaten egg. Bake 25 minutes longer, or until pastry is golden and filling bubbles up. Garnish with parsley, if you wish.

Note—Cut piecrust trimmings into 2-inch lengths; place on a cookie sheet; sprinkle with salt. Bake in hot oven (425°) 8 minutes, or until golden. Serve with soup or salad or as snacks.

Sausage Pizza

Top heat-and-serve pizza with extra meats and cheese—and pop into the oven

Makes 6 servings

1 (12-inch) ready-to-heat pizza
6 slices provolone cheese (from an 8-ounce package)
6 slices salami (from an 8-ounce package)
6 smoked link sausages (from a 10- or 12-ounce package)
1 pepperoni (from a 5-ounce package)
Parsley
2 cups cherry tomatoes

1 Place pizza on ungreased pizza pan or large cookie sheet. Cut cheese slices into quarters; cut salami and sausages in half; slice pepperoni into 18 rounds.
2 Arrange cheese quarters alternately with salami halves, spoke fashion, on top of pizza to make 6 sections; place 2 sausage halves and 2 pepperoni rounds between each near edge. Place 6 pepperoni rounds in a ring in center.
3 Heat, following label directions, or until cheese is bubbly-hot.
4 Place on a large serving tray or platter; cut into 6 wedges; garnish with parsley. Serve with cherry tomatoes.

Hungarian Veal

Mild-flavor veal and autumn vegetables bubble temptingly in a creamy-rich gravy

Bake at 350° for 25 minutes.
Makes 6 servings

1½ pounds lean veal shoulder, cut in cubes
¼ cup sifted all-purpose flour

2 teaspoons salt
⅛ teaspoon pepper
2 tablespoons vegetable oil
1½ cups water
12 small white onions, peeled
1 small eggplant, pared and diced
1 cup dairy sour cream
1 teaspoon paprika
2 cans (2¼ ounces each) shoestring potatoes

1 Shake veal with flour, 1 teaspoon salt and pepper in paper bag to coat well. (Save remaining teaspoon of salt for Step 2.)
2 Brown quickly in vegetable oil in large frying pan; stir in water and remaining teaspoon of salt, then add onions and eggplant. Cover; simmer 30 minutes, or until onions are tender.
3 Stir in sour cream and paprika; spoon mixture into an 8-cup baking dish; sprinkle the potatoes evenly over the top.
4 Bake in moderate oven (350°) 25 minutes, or until meat is tender.

Colonial Chicken

A delicious, broiled chicken that's ready in no time

Broil 30 minutes.
Makes 4 servings

¼ cup buttery-flavor oil
½ teaspoon seasoned salt
¼ teaspoon lemon-pepper seasoning
4 whole chicken breasts, split
1 package (4 ounces) sliced boiled ham
1 can (10½ ounces) chicken gravy
1 can (3 or 4 ounces) sliced mushrooms
1 tablespoon lemon juice

1 Combine oil, salt and pepper seasoning in a cup.
2 Wash and dry chicken breasts; brush both sides with part of oil mixture.
3 Cut ham slices into wide strips.
4 Broil chicken breasts, skin side down, for 15 minutes; turn; brush again.
5 Broil chicken 10 minutes longer. Arrange ham strips on chicken; brush with oil mixture. Broil 5 minutes longer, or until chicken is tender and ham is lightly browned.
6 Heat gravy, mushrooms with liquid and lemon juice until bubbly-hot in a small saucepan.
7 To serve, arrange chicken and ham on small platter; spoon some of gravy mixture over. Serve remaining gravy separately.

CONVENIENCE FOODS AND MIXES MAGIC

If speed is what you are after, then turn to convenience foods and mixes. These turn the last-minute flurry in the kitchen into a relaxed mood. And the result is a delicious, nutritious meal.

Soups, stocks, bread starters, yeast, gelatins, starters of all description—all used to be basic to any good kitchen. But today there is less time for cooking—other than those special occasions. This is where convenience foods and mixes pick up the slack.

And if you place a value on the time away from your hobbies—or the time you don't spend with your surprise guests—then the extra cost of a convenience food or mix becomes a savings.

Here are a few of the most popular:

Biscuit Mixes *Most are now packaged in sizes from 6 ounces to 2½ pounds; especially convenient is a 2-pound box of 8 individual packets, each premeasured to hold just one cup of mix.*

Muffin Mixes *Most packages—corn, blueberry, banana-nut, orange and date-nut—make from 6 to 12 muffins, or, with a little sleight-of-hand, emerge as coffee cake of loaf bread.*

Quick Breads *Most popular is the corn-bread mix in bag or box to bake as a loaf or muffins.*

Yeast Bread and Roll Mixes *These mixes make bread, dinner or sweet rolls, coffee cakes, even pizza crusts.*

Cake Mixes *You can make a different cake every day for weeks without ever repeating. To suit small and large families, cake mixes come in one- and two-layer sizes. And for super convenience, there's a cake-in-a-box that includes frosting.*

Frosting Mixes *These partners to the cake mixes include four basic types: the seven-minute or fluffy; whipped; butter or creamy; ready-to-spread. The seven-minute types need no cooking—you just add boiling water and beat them. To the whipped varieties, add ice water, and then keep the cake chilled, once it's frosted. The butter types call for water plus butter or margarine; the ready-to-spread varieties fill and frost an average two-layer cake or a dozen cupcakes.*

Cooky Mixes *Look for brownie mixes (plain or with nuts), date-bar mix or the plain or chocolate-chip cooky mixes. A gingerbread mix can be turned into drop cookies or rolled cutouts, or happy little gingerbread men to charm the children.*

Piecrust Mixes *The bread sections of some supermarkets carry baked crusts, and many frozen-food cabinets offer unbaked shells, ready to go into the oven. If you prefer crumb crusts, look for them in foil pans, in family and individual tart-shell sizes, and piecrust mixes; in both stick and dry-mix packages.*

Pie Fillings *There are canned fruit fillings; the canned cream types, such as chocolate, vanilla, lemon and pumpkin; canned pie-sliced apples to spice and sweeten to your own taste; and, packaged pie fillings in instant (beat-and-pour) and ready-to-cook forms. Other instants are packaged egg-custard mix and the chiffonlike filling that needs only to be whipped and chilled.*

Soups *These can also double as dips, spreads, and sauces. To packaged, dry-soup mixes, you simply add water and cook. There are also instant broth in jars or tiny envelopes, bouillon cubes, beef extract or concentrate in liquid and paste form.*

Dip Mixes *An envelope of one of these, plus water, milk, dairy sour cream, cream cheese or cottage cheese, and you've a jiffy, expertly blended appetizer.*

Gravy Mixes *Take your pick of dry mixes, liquid, or paste gravy bases. Look for dry mixes in foil envelopes or 5-ounce jars to combine with water, milk or meat drippings.*

Sauce Mixes *Most dry mixes call for water, milk, dairy sour cream, tomato paste or sauce. Some take cooking and others do not, so follow the label directions.*

Meat Seasoners and Marinades *All come in handy packets, boxes or jars and blend spices, herbs and other ingredients that give meats distinctive flavor or extra tenderness. To use instant meat marinade, mix with liquid, pour over meat and let stand at least 15 minutes before cooking.*

Salad-Dressing Mixes *These instants in handy envelopes combine dry herbs and spices. When blended with some vegetable or olive oil, vinegar and water, each packet makes about a cup of dressing to toss with your favorite green salad.*

Cash-Savers For Instants and Mixes Be selective—Look for those products that will give you the most built-in maid service for the least money. You may think the cost of instants and mixes outweighs the convenience. Not so, according to the U.S. Department of Agriculture, which recently studied 158 convenience foods. Its conclusion: 48 convenience foods are cheaper than their less-convenient counterparts, among them instant coffee and devil's-food cake mix.

Consider the shopping time instants and mixes save you—For example, buying a vegetable-soup mix takes one minute, picking out ingredients for a from-scratch soup, 14 minutes. Time saved is money saved.

Cook-Savers Using Instants and Mixes Start with precooked rice or macaroni, or curried, Spanish or Chinese fried-rice mix, add a can of flaked, drained tuna or diced, canned, luncheon meat or diced leftover roast. Mix in sauce made from one of the fancy mixes—sour cream, cheese or onion—and then heat on top of the range or in a moderate oven (350°) just long enough to mellow the flavors.

Country Chicken Casserole

Off the shelf and into a casserole—that's how fast this is to make

Bake at 350° for 1 hour and 30 minutes.
Makes 6 to 8 servings

2 cans (10¾ ounces each) condensed chicken-noodle soup
2 cups milk
1 package (8 ounces) uncooked elbow macaroni
3 cans (about 5 ounces each) boned chicken, diced
1 package (8 ounces) process American cheese, shredded (2 cups)
1 small onion, minced (¼ cup)
4 hard-cooked eggs, shelled and sliced
3 pimientos, drained and chopped
1 teaspoon seasoned salt
⅓ cup grated Parmesan cheese

1 Blend soup and milk until smooth in a 10-cup baking dish. Stir in macaroni, chicken, cheese, onion, eggs, pimientos and salt; cover.
2 Bake in moderate oven (350°) 1 hour and 25 minutes; uncover. Sprinkle with Parmesan cheese. Bake 5 minutes longer, or until cheese is crusty-brown.

Party Chicken

No need to cook all day to enjoy this Southern delicacy—just follow this magic recipe

Bake at 350° for 30 minutes.
Makes 6 to 8 servings

4 chicken legs (drumsticks and thighs)
2 tablespoons all-purpose flour

1 teaspoon salt
⅛ teaspoon pepper
¼ cup vegetable oil
2 packages Spanish-rice mix
1 package (6 to 8 ounces) sliced Italian assortment cold cuts
1 package (5 ounces) frozen cooked deveined shrimps, thawed
2 tablespoons instant chicken bouillon
4 cups hot water

1 Cut chicken legs into drumsticks and thighs; shake in paper bag with flour, salt and pepper to coat evenly.
2 Sauté slowly in vegetable oil in large frying pan 30 minutes, or until fork-tender; place in 10-cup casserole with tight-fitting cover.
3 Sprinkle Spanish rice right from package over chicken; top with sliced meats, then shrimps.
4 Heat chicken bouillon and water to boiling in same frying pan, stirring until bouillon is dissolved; pour over mixture in casserole; cover.
5 Bake in moderate oven (350°) 30 minutes, or until bubbly-hot.

Oven-Crisp Chicken

Onion dip mix gives the crusty crumb coating a zesty flavor lift

Bake at 350° for 1 hour.
Makes 8 servings

2 broiler-fryers (about 2 pounds each), cut up
1 envelope (2 packets) onion dip mix
1 cup soft bread crumbs (2 slices)
1 teaspoon salt
⅛ teaspoon pepper

(continued)

1 Remove skin from chicken, if you wish; cut away small bones from breast pieces.
2 Combine dip mix, bread crumbs, salt and pepper in a paper bag. Shake chicken pieces, a few at a time, in mixture to coat well. Place, not touching, in a single layer in a well-buttered large shallow baking pan.
3 Bake in moderate oven (350°) 1 hour, or until chicken is tender and richly browned.

Salmon Salad Tart

The crust came out of a package and is filled with canned salmon, process American cheese, and out-of-the-bottle stuffed olives, for Salmon Salad Tart

Bake at 450° for 8 minutes,
then at 400° for 20 minutes
Makes 8 servings

6 tablespoons (¾ stick) butter or margarine
1½ cups biscuit mix
¼ cup boiling water
2 cans (1 pound each) salmon
3 hard-cooked eggs, shelled
1 cup thinly sliced celery
¼ cup sliced pimiento-stuffed olives
½ cup mayonnaise or salad dressing
1 package (8 ounces) sliced process American cheese

1 Cut butter or margarine into biscuit mix in a medium-size bowl; stir in boiling water until mixture holds together and leaves side of bowl clean. Place in a 9-inch pie plate.
2 Flour hands and dough lightly, then pat out evenly to make a pastrylike shell and line plate completely; flute edge.
3 Bake in very hot oven (450°) 8 minutes, or until golden. Remove from oven and place on a wire rack; cool slightly. Lower oven temperature to hot (400°).
4 Drain liquid from salmon; remove skin and bones. Break salmon into chunks; place in a large bowl. Cut half of 1 egg into wedges to use for garnish; dice remaining eggs and add to salmon with celery, olives and mayonnaise or salad dressing; toss lightly to mix.
5 Cut block of cheese in half diagonally; separate into 8 double triangles; stand around edge in shell. Spoon in salmon mixture. Cover loosely with foil.
6 Bake in hot oven (400°) 20 minutes, or until filling is hot. Garnish with egg wedges. Cut in wedges; serve warm.

Tuna with Mushroom Sauce

Kids will love this special way to serve a favorite food

Bake at 400° for 20 minutes.
Makes 4 servings

2 cans (7 ounces each) tuna, drained and flaked
1 medium-size onion, sliced in thin rings
1 green pepper, seeded and sliced in thin strips
2 teaspoons finely chopped parsley
1 can (10¾ ounces) condensed cream of mushroom soup
1 can (10½ ounces) cream of mushroom soup
½ soup-can water
½ teaspoon salt
⅛ teaspoon pepper
½ cup shredded process American cheese

1 Grease a 6-cup casserole and in it make layers of tuna, onion, pepper and parsley.
2 Dilute soup with water; add salt and pepper and pour over layers in casserole. Sprinkle cheese over top.
3 Bake approximately 20 minutes in hot oven (400°).

Smorgasbord Tuna Salad

A pretty-to-look-at and satisfying-to-eat main dish salad

Makes 6 servings

1 can (1 pound) small white potatoes, drained
1 can (1 pound) cut wax beans, drained
6 tablespoons bottled oil-and-vinegar salad dressing
6 large romaine leaves
2 cans (about 7 ounces each) tuna, drained and broken in chunks
1 can (1 pound) tomato wedges, drained
1 tablespoon capers, drained
Freshly ground black pepper

1 Slice potatoes into a medium-size bowl; place beans in a second bowl. Drizzle each with 2 tablespoons of the salad dressing; toss lightly to mix.
2 Line a large salad bowl with romaine; place tuna in center. Pile potatoes, beans and tomatoes in sections around tuna; sprinkle capers over tuna.
3 Drizzle remaining 2 tablespoons salad dressing over tomatoes; sprinkle pepper over all.

The background may be slow—old-time Clippers—but the fish and seafood is fast put together.

Tuna Potpie

Refrigerated biscuits make a quick top for this tuna-vegetable mixture

Bake at 400° for 12 minutes.

Makes 6 servings

3 carrots, sliced
1 small onion, diced (¼ cup)
½ cup sliced celery
¼ cup diced green pepper
1 bay leaf
1 can (10¾ ounces) condensed cream of mushroom soup
½ soup-can water
1 can (8 ounces) peas
2 cans (7 ounces each) tuna, drained and flaked
1 package refrigerated biscuits

1 In a medium-size saucepan put the carrots, onion, celery, green pepper and bay leaf, with enough water to barely cover. Bring to boiling and cook until just tender; remove bay leaf; drain. Mix soup and water in a medium-size saucepan; heat until bubbly-hot; add drained vegetables along with peas and tuna. Pour into a greased 6-cup shallow baking dish; top with biscuits. Bake in hot oven (400°) 12 minutes, or until biscuits are golden brown.

Tuna Divan

This busy-day dinner-in-a-dish features tuna and broccoli in a vegetable-soup sauce

Makes 4 servings

2 packages (10 ounces each) frozen broccoli spears
1 can(10½ ounces) condensed vegetable soup
¼ cup milk
1 can (about 7 ounces) tuna, drained and flaked
2 tablespoons grated Parmesan cheese

1 Cook broccoli by package directions; drain.
2 Heat soup and milk in small saucepan; beat until smooth.

(continued)

3 Arrange broccoli in shallow broilerproof dish; top with tuna; pour sauce over; sprinkle with cheese.
4 Slide under broiler, about 4 inches from heat, until bubbly-hot.

Tuna Roly-Poly

Practically everything for this dish is an "on hand" from your cupboard shelf

Bake at 400° about 15 minutes.

Makes 4 servings

2 cups biscuit mix
⅔ cup milk
1 can (about 7 ounces) tuna, drained and flaked
1 cup finely diced celery
¼ cup diced stuffed green olives
¼ cup mayonnaise or salad dressing
2 tablespoons dairy sour cream
MUSHROOM SAUCE (recipe follows)

1 Combine biscuit mix and milk in medium-size bowl; mix, following label directions for plain biscuits. Roll or pat out to a rectangle, 8x10, on lightly floured pastry cloth or board.
2 Mix tuna, celery, olives, mayonnaise or salad dressing, and sour cream in medium-size bowl; spread evenly over dough. Beginning at one end, roll up, jelly-roll fashion; pinch edges together to seal.
3 Slice crosswise into 8 even-size pieces; place, not touching, on a greased cookie sheet.
4 Bake in hot oven (400°) 15 minutes, or until golden. Serve with MUSHROOM SAUCE.
MUSHROOM SAUCE—Combine 1 can (10½ ounces) condensed cream of mushroom soup and ⅓ cup milk in small saucepan. Heat to boiling; stir in 1 tablespoon cut chives. Makes about 1½ cups.

Stuffed Pancakes Newburg

Try this as a party dish

Makes 6 servings

2 packages (8 ounces each) frozen pancakes
2 cups (1 pound) cream-style cottage cheese

1 small cucumber, pared, seeded, and chopped (⅔ cup)
1 tablespoon grated onion
¼ tablespoon Worcestershire sauce
⅛ teaspoon salt
NEWBURG SHRIMP SAUCE (recipe follows)

1 Let pancakes stand in opened package until thawed enough to separate.
2 Combine cottage cheese, cucumber, onion, Worcestershire sauce and salt in medium-size bowl; spread between pancakes to make 6 sandwiches; place on cookie sheet.
3 Bake in moderate oven (350°) 20 to 30 minutes, or until cheese filling is hot; remove from oven; cut in half; serve with NEWBURG SHRIMP SAUCE.

NEWBURG SHRIMP SAUCE—Combine 1 can (10¾ ounces) condensed cream of shrimp soup, 1 package (5 ounces) thawed, frozen ready-to-eat shrimp, ¼ cup milk, and 2 tablespoons chopped parsley in medium size saucepan; cook over medium heat, stirring until smooth and bubbly. Season with 2 teaspoons sherry, if you wish.

Deep-Sea Bake

Unfold each hot foil bundle and the main course of your dinner is ready

Makes 6 servings

2 packages (12 ounces each) frozen perch, haddock, cod or flounder fillets
6 tablespoons (¾ stick) butter or margarine
1 large onion, chopped (1 cup)
3 large potatoes, cooked, peeled, and sliced
2 teaspoons salt
1 teaspoon paprika
1 package (10 ounces) frozen whole-kernel corn

1 Cut each package of frozen fish fillets into 3 equal-size servings (no need to thaw).
2 Melt butter or margarine in small saucepan; stir in onion; heat just until bubbly.
3 Have ready six 12-inch squares of heavy aluminum foil. Place about 1 tablespoon butter mixture on each; top with a serving of fish, more onion-butter mixture then potatoes, dividing evenly. Sprinkle all with salt and paprika; top with frozen corn. Fold and seal foil into bundles with a drugstore wrap.
4 Cook on grill over hot coals, turning every 15 minutes, 1 hour, or until fish flakes easily with a fork. Serve in foil wrappers.

Mandarin Shrimps

Frozen shrimps and vegetables go, Far Eastern fashion, in and out of the frying pan fast

Makes 6 servings

3 tablespoons vegetable oil
1 bag (1½ pounds) frozen deveined shelled raw shrimps
1 clove of garlic, crushed
1 package (about 10 ounces) frozen green beans and mushrooms
1 can (5 ounces) water chestnuts, drained and sliced
1 can (10¾ ounces) condensed chicken broth
¼ teaspoon ground ginger
2 cans (about 11 ounces each) fried rice
2 tablespoons cornstarch
½ cup water
2 tablespoons soy sauce

1 Heat oil quickly in a large frying pan; stir in frozen shrimps and garlic. Sauté 5 minutes; push to one side.
2 Place frozen green beans and mushrooms in pan; heat, breaking vegetables apart as they thaw, 3 minutes; stir in water chestnuts, chicken broth and ginger; cover. Simmer 10 minutes.
3 While shrimp mixture simmers, heat fried rice, following the label directions.
4 Smooth cornstarch and water to a paste in a cup; stir in soy sauce, then stir into shrimp mixture. Cook slowly, stirring constantly, until the mixture thickens and boils 3 minutes.
5 Spoon rice around edge of a large deep serving bowl; spoon shrimp mixture in center. Garnish with sprigs of parsley, if you wish.

Skillet Paella

With canned and packaged foods you can create this Spanish dish in no time

Makes 6 servings

1 can (1 pound) green peas
1 can (about 5 ounces) boned chicken
1 large onion, chopped (1 cup)
1 clove garlic, chopped
1 tablespoon vegetable oil
2 cups packaged precooked rice
1 can (1 pound) stewed tomatoes
1 can (4 or 5 ounces) Vienna sausages, drained and sliced
¼ teaspoon leaf thyme, crumbled

⅛ teaspoon pepper
2 cans (5 ounces each) deveined shrimps, drained and rinsed

1 Drain liquids from peas and chicken into a 2-cup measure; add water to make 1½ cups. Dice chicken.
2 Sauté onion and garlic in vegetable oil until soft in a large frying pan; stir in rice, tomatoes and the 1½ cups liquid. Heat to boiling; stir in peas, chicken, sausages, thyme and pepper; place shrimps on top; cover.
3 Simmer 10 minutes, or until rice is tender and liquid is absorbed. Just before serving, sprinkle with chopped parsley, if you wish.

Fish-and-Shells Italiano

Flavorful cod and tender macaroni shells bake in a zippy-rich tomato sauce

Bake at 375° for 30 minutes.
Makes 6 servings

1 package (1 pound) macaroni shells
1 medium-size onion, chopped (½ cup)
½ teaspoon leaf basil, crumbled
2 tablespoons olive oil
1 envelope spaghetti-sauce mix
1 can (about 2 pounds) Italian tomatoes
1 package (1 pound) frozen cod fillets, cut into cubes
⅓ cup grated Parmesan cheese
1 package (8 ounces) sliced mozzarella cheese

1 Cook macaroni shells, following label directions; drain.
2 While shells cook, sauté onion with basil in olive oil in large saucepan; stir in spaghetti-sauce mix and tomatoes. Cover; simmer 10 minutes; add fish cubes; simmer 10 minutes longer.
3 Spoon half the macaroni shells into a 12-cup casserole; sprinkle with half the Parmesan cheese; top with half the fish-tomato sauce. Repeat layers; arrange mozzarella-cheese slices on top.
4 Bake in moderate oven (375°) 30 minutes, or until bubbly-hot.
Note—If made in the morning and chilled, take from refrigerator and let stand at room temperature 30 minutes before putting into oven to bake.

Shrimp and Noodles au Gratin

Meatless meals are a breeze, when they are as easy to do as this

Bake at 350° for 20 minutes.
Makes 4 generous servings

1 package noodles with sour cream and cheese sauce mix
Milk
Butter or margarine
1 package (1 pound) frozen shelled deveined shrimp
1 can (3 or 4 ounces) sliced mushrooms, drained
1 carton (8 ounces) cottage cheese
½ teaspoon dillweed
3 tablespoons fine dry bread crumbs
1 tablespoon butter or margarine, softened

1 Prepare noodles with milk and butter or margarine in a medium-size saucepan, following label directions.
2 Cook shrimp in a medium-size saucepan, following label directions; drain and chop. Add to noodle mixture.
3 Stir in mushrooms, cottage cheese and dillweed. Spoon into a 6-cup casserole.
4 Combine bread crumbs and butter or margarine in a small bowl. Sprinkle over casserole.
5 Bake in moderate oven (350°) 20 minutes, or until casserole is bubbly-hot.

Spaghetti with Clam Sauce

Friday way with spaghetti—and ready in minutes

Makes 6 servings

1 package (1 pound) thin spaghetti
2 cloves of garlic, minced
½ cup (1 stick) butter or margarine
4 cans (7 ounces each) minced clams
2 teaspoons lemon juice
Dash of cayenne pepper

1 Cook spaghetti, following label directions; drain; keep hot in kettle.
2 While spaghetti cooks, sauté garlic lightly in butter or margarine in medium-size saucepan. Stir in remaining ingredients; simmer 5 minutes.
3 Toss with hot spaghetti; serve plain or with your favorite grated cheese.

Macaroni-Tuna Subs

This knife-and-fork whopper starts with ready-to-heat canned macaroni

Makes 4 servings

2 cans (about 1 pound each) macaroni in cheese sauce
1 can (about 7 ounces) tuna, drained and flaked
2 tablespoons sweet-pickle relish
1 teaspoon Worcestershire sauce
4 toasted split hamburger buns
Dried chopped parsley

1 Combine macaroni in cheese sauce, tuna, relish and Worcestershire sauce in a medium-size saucepan; heat slowly, stirring often, 5 minutes, or until hot.
2 Spoon over toasted buns; sprinkle with parsley. Serve hot.

Presto Lasagna

The fastest recipe we know for this favorite Italian dish—and it's so good!

Bake at 350° for 30 minutes.
Makes 4 servings

1 package (8 ounces) regular noodles
1 tablespoon vegetable oil or olive oil
1 package (8 ounces) heat-and-serve sausage patties
1 can (about 1 pound) Italian tomatoes
1 can (8 ounces) tomato sauce
1 tablespoon instant minced onion
1 teaspoon mixed Italian herbs
1 carton (8 ounces) pot cheese
¼ cup grated Parmesan cheese
1 package (6 or 8 ounces) sliced mozzarella cheese, cut into ½-inch strips

1 Cook noodles, following label directions; drain; return to same kettle; toss with salad oil or olive oil to keep from sticking.
2 While noodles cook, dice sausage patties; brown with no fat, stirring often, in medium-size frying pan; stir in tomatoes, tomato sauce, onion and herbs; heat to boiling; simmer, stirring often, 5 minutes.

3 Layer half the noodles, pot cheese, Parmesan cheese, tomato mixture and mozzarella cheese in 6-cup shallow baking dish; repeat, criss-crossing mozzarella strips on top.
4 Bake in moderate oven (350°) 30 minutes, or until bubbling at edges and cheese is lightly browned; remove from oven; let stand 5 to 10 minutes to set.
Note—For a party, double the recipe and bake in 12-cup shallow baking dish at 350° until bubbly-hot.

Pinwheel Lasagna

Flexible food, the lasagna noodle! Here you roll it with a two-cheese filling

Bake at 350° for 45 minutes.
Makes 6 servings

12 *lasagne noodles (from a 1-pound package)*
2 *cups (1-pound carton) cream-style cottage cheese*
1 *package (3 or 4 ounces) cream cheese*
2 *eggs*
¼ *cup chopped parsley*
1 *teaspoon leaf basil, crumbled*
½ *teaspoon salt*
1 *jar (1 pound) meatless spaghetti sauce*
1 *package (8 ounces) sliced mozzarella or pizza cheese*

1 Slide lasagne noodles, one at a time, into a kettle of boiling salted water. Cook, following label directions; drain; return to kettle. Cover with cold water.
2 Combine cottage and cream cheeses in a medium-size bowl; beat in eggs, parsley, basil and salt.
3 Lift noodles, one at a time, from water; drain on paper toweling. Spread with ¼ cup of the cheese filling; roll up, jelly-roll fashion.
4 Place, seam-side down, in a large shallow baking dish; spoon spaghetti sauce over rolls; cover dish.
5 Bake in moderate oven (350°) 40 minutes; uncover. Cut mozzarella or pizza cheese into strips; arrange over rolls in dish. Bake 5 minutes longer, or until cheese melts.

SALAD

Crab Salad

Serve as an appetizer, California style, or spoon into lettuce cups for a main-dish salad

Makes 4 servings

1 *package (about 6 ounces) frozen king crab-meat, thawed and drained*
½ *cup diced celery*
2 *tablespoons bottled Italian-style dressing*
4 *dashes liquid red pepper seasoning*
Parsley
4 *lemon wedges*

1 Cut crabmeat into medium-size chunks, carefully removing any bony tissue; combine with celery in a small bowl.
2 Sprinkle with salad dressing and pepper seasoning; toss to mix well.
3 Serve in small scallop-shell-shape dishes or salad plates; garnish with parsley and a lemon wedge.
Note—Double this recipe for a main-dish salad to be served in lettuce cups.

Western Salmon Salad Bowl

Golden pineapple tidbits add sparkle to this West Coast favorite

Makes 4 servings

1 *can (1 pound) salmon*
1 *can (8¼ ounces) pineapple chunks, drained*
1½ *cups chopped celery*
2 *tablespoons grated onion*
2 *tablespoons lemon juice*
Few drops bottled red pepper seasoning
OLD-FASHIONED BOILED DRESSING *(recipe follows)*
1 *small head iceberg lettuce*
Lemon wedges

1 Drain salmon; flake into large pieces, removing any small bones and skin.
2 Combine pineapple chunks, celery, onion, lemon juice, red pepper seasoning, and ½ cup OLD-FASHIONED BOILED DRESSING in medium-size bowl. Fold in flaked salmon; cover; chill.
3 Edge salad bowl with a few lettuce leaves; chop remaining lettuce and place in bottom.

(continued)

Spoon salad mixture on top; garnish with lemon wedges. Pass remaining dressing.

OLD-FASHIONED BOILED DRESSING—Mix 2 tablespoons flour, 1 tablespoon sugar, 1 teaspoon salt, 1 teaspoon dry mustard, ¼ teaspoon ground ginger and a dash of cayenne in top of double boiler. Beat in ¾ cup milk and 1 egg until well blended. Cook over simmering water, stirring constantly, 10 minutes, or until mixture thickens. Remove from heat; gradually blend in ¼ cup cider vinegar. Pour into a small bowl; cover; chill. Makes about 1 cup.

German Potato Salad

This old-fashioned winner goes modern with quick-fix potatoes and lots of crisp bacon chips in a hot spicy dressing

Makes 6 servings

½ pound (about 12 slices) bacon, cut in ½-inch pieces
1 package (1 pound) frozen French fried potatoes
1 cup chopped celery
2 tablespoons cider vinegar
2 tablespoons brown sugar
½ teaspoon salt
Dash of pepper

1 Sauté bacon until crisp in a large frying pan; drain on paper toweling.
2 Cook potatoes in same pan, following label directions for pan-frying; drain on paper toweling. Cut into bite-size pieces and combine with bacon and celery in a salad bowl.
3 Pour off all drippings, then measure 2 tablespoonfuls and return to pan; stir in remaining ingredients. Heat to boiling; then simmer 1 minute. Pour over potato mixture; toss to mix well. Serve warm.

Salad Nicoise

A refreshingly simple salad that may be prepared earlier in the day, then assembled and served

Makes 6 servings.

5 medium-size potatoes, cooked, drained and cooled
½ pound fresh green beans, cooked, drained and cooled
⅔ cup vegetable oil
⅓ cup wine vinegar
2 cloves garlic, crushed
1 tablespoon prepared mustard
1 tablespoon chopped parsley
½ teaspoon instant minced onion
1 teaspoon salt
¼ teaspoon ground pepper
2 large tomatoes, cut into wedges
1 red onion, cubed
1 small green pepper, seeded and cubed
6 ripe olives, halved
3 hard-cooked eggs, shelled and sliced
1 can (2 ounces) anchovy fillets, drained
2 medium-size heads of romaine
1 can (14 ounces) tuna fish, drained

1 Peel potatoes and cut into thick slices. Place in a shallow dish. Place beans in a second dish.
2 Combine oil, vinegar, garlic, mustard, parsley, onion, salt and pepper in a jar with a tight-fitting lid; shake well to mix. Drizzle ½ cup over potatoes and 2 tablespoons over beans; let each stand at least 30 minutes to season.
3 Layer vegetables, eggs, anchovies and romaine in a large salad bowl. Break tuna into chunks; arrange on top. Pour rest of dressing over; toss.

Hungarian Bean Bowl

Red and white kidney beans dressed with peppy seasoned sour cream make this unusual casserole-salad

Makes 6 to 8 servings

1 can (about 1 pound) red kidney beans
1 can (about 1 pound) white kidney beans
2 tablespoons vegetable oil
2 tablespoons cider vinegar
2 tablespoons chopped parsley
2 teaspoons sugar
1 envelope garlic-olive dip mix
1 small head of iceberg lettuce, shredded
½ cup dairy sour cream
1 can (about 3 ounces) French fried onion rings

1 Drain red and white kidney beans well; place beans in a large bowl.
2 Drizzle with vegetable oil and vinegar; sprinkle with parsley, sugar and dip mix; toss to mix well. Cover; chill at least an hour to season and blend flavors. (Or let stand at room temperature if you prefer salad not too chilled.)
3 When ready to serve, place shredded lettuce

in a large casserole or bowl. Stir sour cream into bean mixture; spoon on top of lettuce; sprinkle with onion rings.

Yankee Doodle Salad

Popular macaroni and cheese with a new twist —and a main dish and salad in one

Makes 4 servings

1 can (about 1 pound) macaroni in cheese sauce
½ pound unsliced bologna, cubed
1 cup sliced celery
½ cup chopped sweet pickles
2 tablespoons mayonnaise or salad dressing
1 teaspoon dry mustard
1 head iceberg lettuce, quartered

1 Combine all ingredients, except lettuce, in medium-size bowl; toss lightly with a fork to mix. (If made ahead, chill until serving time.)
2 Spoon generously over lettuce wedges. Serve plain or with sliced tomatoes, if you wish.

Marinated Bean and Chestnut Bowl

Water chestnuts give a delightful crunch and texture to this salad

Makes 4 servings

1 can (1 pound) sliced green beans, drained
¼ cup sliced water chestnuts
½ cup halved cherry tomatoes
½ cup oil and vinegar dressing
2 teaspoons minced onion
1 teaspoon parsley flakes
½ teaspoon leaf basil, crumbled
1 small head iceberg lettuce

1 Combine beans, water chestnuts and halved tomatoes in a medium-size bowl.
2 Combine dressing, onion, parsley and basil in a jar with a tight lid; cover; shake until well blended.
3 Pour dressing over vegetables; cover. Marinate in refrigerator 3 hours.
4 Break lettuce into a salad bowl.
5 Drain vegetables; spoon into lettuce-lined bowl.

Grapefruit-Cucumber Toss

No need to peel and section grapefruit—just use the convenient jarred sections

Makes 4 servings

4 cups broken romaine
2 cups broken endive
1 small cucumber
2 cups drained unsweetened grapefruit sections (from a 32-ounce jar)
½ cup bottled Russian dressing

1 Arrange greens in a salad bowl.
2 Score cucumber and slice thin; arrange on top of lettuce in a ring; spoon grapefruit sections in center.
3 Just before serving, drizzle dressing over; toss to coat well.

A collection of main-dish accompaniments, and all are made with convenience foods.

Salad Corn Mingle

A colorful vegetable salad with a tang from pickle relish

Makes 8 servings

2 cans (12 ounces each) Mexican-style corn
1 can (1 pound) Italian green beans
5 large radishes, trimmed
    and chopped
½ cup mayonnaise or salad dressing
2 tablespoons sweet-pickle relish, drained
1 teaspoon lemon juice
½ teaspoon salt
    Iceberg lettuce

1 Drain liquids from corn and beans; combine vegetables with radishes in a medium-size bowl.
2 Blend mayonnaise or salad dressing, pickle relish, lemon juice and salt in a small bowl; fold into vegetable mixture. Serve in a lettuce-lined bowl.

Lima Salad Cups

They double as a vegetable, travel well, need no chilling

Makes 6 servings

2 packages (10 ounces each) frozen Fordhook
    lima beans
2 cups sliced celery
¼ cup thin French dressing
¼ pound unsliced process American cheese,
    cut in small cubes
1 pimiento, diced
    Lettuce

1 Cook lima beans, following label directions, adding celery during last 5 minutes' cooking; drain; place in medium-size bowl.
2 Pour French dressing over; toss lightly to mix; cool.
3 Just before serving, add cheese and pimiento; toss lightly. Serve in lettuce-lined cups or bowls.

Spinach Salad Imperial

Maple-flavor bacon gives this a country taste

Makes 8 servings

1 package (10 ounces) fresh spinach
¼ pound sliced maple-flavor bacon, cut in 1-
    inch pieces

1 large carrot, pared and shredded
⅓ cup bottled oil-and-vinegar salad dressing
4 slices process white American cheese, cut
    in small squares
1 cup onion-ring snacks

1 Trim stems and any coarse ribs from spinach. Wash leaves and drain well. Break or cut into bite-size pieces; place in a large salad bowl.
2 Sauté bacon until crisp in a medium-size frying pan; remove and drain on paper toweling.
3 Just before serving, add carrot to spinach; drizzle dressing over top; toss lightly to mix. Stack cheese and bacon in center; sprinkle onion rings over all.

Wilted Cabbage Slaw

All slaw lovers will go for this one with a new twist

Makes 4 servings

4 cups shredded cabbage (½ small head)
1 cup shredded carrot (1 large)
½ cup sliced celery
1 small onion, sliced
1 envelope Italian salad dressing mix
    Vinegar
    Water
    Vegetable oil

1 Combine cabbage, carrot, celery and sliced onion in a medium-size bowl.
2 Prepare salad dressing mix with vinegar, water and oil, following label directions.
3 Heat ½ cup of the prepared dressing just to boiling; pour over vegetables; toss lightly. Refrigerate remaining dressing to use for salads at other meals.

Buffet Mold

Make this the star of your next party

Makes 6 to 8 servings

2 envelopes unflavored gelatin
2¾ cups cold water
1 can (6 ounces) frozen concentrated orange
    juice
¼ cup sugar
⅛ teaspoon salt
2 tablespoons lemon juice
½ cup shredded carrot
½ cup finely chopped celery

1 cup cottage cheese
1 can (9 ounces) crushed pineapple, drained

1 Soften gelatin in ½ cup cold water in top of double boiler; dissolve over hot water; remove from heat.
2 Stir in orange juice, 2¼ cups water, sugar, salt and lemon juice; divide in half; chill one half until syrupy; keep other half at room temperature for Step 4.
3 Fold carrot and celery into syrupy gelatin; pour into 6-cup mold; chill until almost set. (Gelatin layer should be slightly sticky so second layer will mold to it as it chills.)
4 Chill second half of gelatin until syrupy; fold in cottage cheese and pineapple; spoon carefully on top of almost-firm gelatin; chill 2 to 3 hours, or until firm. Unmold; serve plain or with dressing.

Grapefruit-Aspic Mold

This beauty can be served as a salad or as a relish

Makes 6 servings

2 cans (1 pound each) grapefruit sections
　Water
1 package (6 ounces) lemon-flavor gelatin
2 cans (8 ounces each) tomato sauce
　Few drops liquid red pepper seasoning

1 Drain syrup from grapefruit into a 2-cup measure. (Set grapefruit aside for Step 3.) Add water to syrup to make 2 cups; heat to boiling in small saucepan.
2 Pour over gelatin in a medium-size bowl, stirring until gelatin dissolves. Stir in tomato sauce and liquid red pepper seasoning until well blended. Chill about 30 minutes, or until as thick as unbeaten egg white.
3 Fold in grapefruit sections; spoon into a 6-cup mold. Chill several hours, or until firm.
4 To unmold, run a sharp-tip thin-blade knife around top of mold, then dip mold *very quickly* in and out of a pan of hot water. Cover mold with serving plate; turn upside down; carefully lift off mold.
5 Serve plain as a relish, or as a salad garnished with watercress or small inner leaves of romaine. Pass your favorite mayonnaise or salad dressing in a separate bowl.

Ham Mousse in Aspic

Shimmering beef aspic sparkles around a smooth creamy ham mousse—a perfect party make-ahead

Makes 6 servings.

2 cans condensed beef broth
3 envelopes unflavored gelatin
2½ cups diced cooked ham
1 can (3¾ ounces) liver pâté
1 tablespoon prepared mustard with horse-radish
　Red food coloring (optional)
1 cup heavy cream, whipped
6 thin slices cooked ham
　Pimiento
　Celery tops
　Parsley

1 Empty beef broth into a 4-cup measure; add enough water to make 4 cups. Sprinkle gelatin over 1 cup of broth mixture in small saucepan; let soften 5 minutes. Heat slowly, stirring constantly, until gelatin is completely dissolved; add to remaining beef broth. Pour 1 cup into a 9x9x2-inch baking pan; chill until set (for decorating platter).
2 Whirl diced ham with 1¾ cups of remaining gelatin mixture, ⅓ at a time, in container of electric blender until smooth. Turn into a large bowl; stir in liver pâté, mustard and enough red food coloring to tint slightly pink, if you wish. Chill mixture until it is thick enough to mound softly when spooned; fold in whipped cream. (This is the ham mousse.)
3 Meanwhile, roll the thin ham slices into cone shapes; fit inside foil cones (*directions follow*). Refrigerate. Pour about ⅓ cup gelatin into a 5-cup ring mold; set in a pan of ice and water (chill remaining gelatin until syrupy). When almost set or sticky-firm, arrange cutouts of pimiento and celery or parsley leaves on gelatin; spoon about ¼ cup of the chilled syrupy gelatin over and around decorations.
4 Spoon ham mousse into a pastry bag fitted with a large notched tip; pipe mousse into cones to fill them; place on a rack so they won't roll around; chill. Pipe a generous layer of mousse on top of the gelatin in mold, leaving a space next to side of mold. Spoon remaining gelatin down side of mold, then pipe in remaining mousse; smooth out top. Chill several hours, or until completely set.
5 To unmold: Loosen around edges with a small knife; dip mold quickly in and out of a pan of hot water. Cover with serving plate; turn upside

(continued)

down; shake gently to release mousse; lift off mold. Remove filled cones from foil molds. Arrange cones in center of mold with parsley.
6 Cut gelatin in square pan into cubes; spoon around mold. Keep refrigerated until ready to serve.

FOIL CONES—For each cone, tear off a 6-inch piece of heavy-duty foil from an 18-inch-wide roll. Fold each piece in thirds to make a square; fold crosswise to make a triangle. Using center of longest side of triangle as tip of cone, start at one side and roll up to form a cone.

Hero Salad

This economical sandwich-in-a salad bowl can be made from almost any combination of your favorite coldcuts, or cheeses

Makes about 6 servings.

1 large head Boston lettuce, broken
½ pound sliced salami
¼ pound sliced ham
¼ pound sliced bologna
½ pound Swiss cheese
1 green pepper, sliced
1 red pepper, sliced
Hot red cherry peppers (from a 16-ounce jar)
Italian-style pickled green peppers (from a 12-ounce jar)
Oil-cured olives (from an 8-ounce jar)
Oil-and-vinegar dressing

Arrange lettuce around edge of salad bowl. Add all remaining ingredients (except dressing), following arrangement in photograph on page 21. Then drizzle with dressing, or let everyone make up individual salad plates and add dressing to taste. Serve with crusty French or Italian bread.

Chicken Pasta Picnic Bowl

A colorful macaroni salad that uses the smaller pieces of chicken

Makes 6 to 8 servings.

1 package (8 ounces) elbow macaroni
1 package (10 ounces) frozen peas and carrots
2 cups diced cooked chicken
1 cup diced Cheddar cheese
½ cup sliced celery
½ cup vegetable oil

⅓ cup tarragon vinegar
1 teaspoon salt
½ teaspoon sugar
½ teaspoon leaf marjoram, crumbled
¼ teaspoon dry mustard
¼ teaspoon pepper
2 tablespoons chopped parsley
2 tablespoons chopped green onion

1 Cook macaroni following label directions; drain; rinse in cold water and drain again.
2 Cook peas and carrots, following package directions, until barely tender. Drain; cool, then add to macaroni in large bowl. Add chicken, cheese and celery.
3 Combine remaining ingredients in jar with tight-fitting lid; shake vigorously until blended. Pour dressing over macaroni mixture; toss well. Chill several hours or overnight.
4 Serve with crisp lettuce and garnish with tomatoes, if you wish.

DESSERTS FROM MIXES

Gâteau de Poires Helene

The famous Poires Helene combine with delicate angel cake to make this delightful creation

Preparation time: 12 minutes.
Makes 12 servings.

1 eight to nine-inch baker's angel food cake
1 can (1 pound) pear halves
¼ cup crème de cacao
2 containers (6¾ ounces each) frozen whipped topping dessert, thawed
1 can (5 ounces) vanilla pudding
1 cup flaked coconut
Fudge topping (from an 11-ounce jar)
Toasted coconut (optional)

1 Split cake horizontally into 3 layers. Drain pears. Combine 2 tablespoons of the juice with crème de cacao, drizzle over cake layers.
2 Press about 1 cup of the whipped topping into a medium-size bowl; stir in vanilla pudding and flaked coconut. Then spread this filling on two of the cake layers.
3 Stack filled layers with plain layer on top, on

serving plate. Arrange pear halves with narrow ends to the center on top layer.

4 Pipe remaining whipped topping onto side of cake and between pears on top. Just before serving, spoon fudge topping over the pears. To top off the cake, sprinkle with toasted coconut, if you wish.

NOTE: To toast coconut, spread 2 tablespoons coconut onto small cooky sheet; place in slow oven (325°) about 8 to 10 minutes.

Easy Cheese Fruit Tarts

Tiny nibbles of delicious fruit and cheese—so easy to put together with the new quick-dessert supermarket items.

Preparation time: 5 minutes.
Chilling time: 30 minutes.
Makes 6 servings.

2 packages (3 ounces each) cream cheese
½ cup milk
1 can (9¾ ounces) raspberry or pineapple
    dessert mix
1 package (5 ounces) pastry tart shells (6 to
    a package)
    Fresh or canned fruits for garnish
    Chopped pistachio nuts or almonds

1 Beat cream cheese until soft in a small bowl. Gradually beat in milk; continue beating until completely smooth. Add dessert mix; stir with a spoon 30 seconds, or until thickened.
2 Spoon into tart shells, dividing evenly. Decorate with fruits of your choice; sprinkle with nuts, if you wish. Chill until ready to serve.

Black-Bottom Rum Pie

No baking necessary for this delicious morsel, just mix and chill

Preparation time: 20 minutes.
Chilling time: Several hours.
Makes one eight-inch pie.

2 cans (5 ounces each) vanilla pudding
2 cans (5 ounces each) chocolate pudding
2 tablespoons rum
1 envelope unflavored gelatin
¼ cup water
1 eight or nine-inch prepared graham cracker
    pie shell

1 container (9 ounces) non-dairy whipped top-
    ping
    Chocolate curls

1 Place vanilla pudding in a small bowl; combine chocolate pudding and rum in another small bowl, reserve.
2 Soften gelatin in the water in a 1-cup measure. Place over hot, not boiling, water in a small saucepan until gelatin dissolves.
3 Stir 2 tablespoons of the dissolved gelatin into the vanilla pudding; add remaining gelatin mixture to chocolate-rum mixture. Place bowl containing chocolate-rum mixture in a pan of ice and water to speed-set. Chill, stirring often, until it is as thick as an unbeaten egg white; pour into prepared graham cracker pie shell.
4 Add 1 cup non-dairy whipped topping into vanilla pudding mixture; fold in carefully; pile on top of chocolate mixture; chill in refrigerator several hours until firm.
5 To serve: Decorate with remaining non-dairy whipped topping and chocolate curls.

Peach Melba Bavarian

With the electric blender doing the work, your cool shimmering dessert is ready to mold and chill in minutes

Preparation time: 10 minutes.
Chilling time: Several hours.
Makes 8 servings.

1 package (3 ounces) lemon-flavored gelatin
1 envelope unflavored gelatin
¼ cup cold milk
1 cup boiling water
2 egg yolks
⅓ cup sugar
    Dash of salt
2 tablespoons peach brandy
1 package (10 ounces) frozen peach slices, cut
    into small pieces
1 cup heavy cream
    Bottled raspberry sundae topping

1 Combine lemon-flavored gelatin and unflavored gelatin in the container of an electric blender; pour cold milk over and allow to stand 1 minute.
2 Pour boiling water into container; cover; whirl at low speed 2 minutes; remove cover. Add egg yolks, sugar, salt and peach brandy.
3 Replace blender cover and remove feeder cap. Whirl at high speed, gradually adding

(continued)

pieces of frozen peaches until mixture is smooth. Add cream if you have room in container; whirl until well-blended. (If you don't have room, stir with a rubber scraper until cream is well-blended.)

4 Pour mixture into a 5-cup ring mold. Chill at least 2 hours before serving.

5 To serve: Run a thin-bladed knife around edges of mold. Dip mold quickly in and out of a pan of hot water. Invert onto serving plate. Spoon bottled raspberry topping over.

Coffee Parfait Pie

When your next party needs a special dessert, try this pie that tastes like a million, with looks to match

> Preparation time: 10 minutes.
> Chilling time: 1 hour.
> Makes 8 to 10 servings.

3 pints coffee ice cream
3 envelopes unflavored gelatin
⅓ cup golden rum
1 tablespoon instant coffee
⅔ cup water
1 eight- or nine-inch prepared graham cracker pie shell
Chocolate syrup
Pecan halves

1 Remove ice cream from freezer to room temperature.

2 Sprinkle gelatin into rum in a 1-cup measure to soften for 5 minutes.

3 Combine instant coffee and water in a small saucepan, bring to boiling. Add softened gelatin; stir until completely dissolved.

4 Turn ice cream into a large bowl. Beat with electric mixer at high speed, until smooth. Pour gelatin in, all at once, while beating constantly and guiding mixture into beater with rubber spatula. (Mixture sets softly, almost at once.)

5 Spoon into pie shell, mounding high in center, or pipe through a pastry bag fitted with a decorative tip, as pictured. Chill until ready to serve. Just before serving, drizzle chocolate syrup over top and garnish with pecans, if you wish.

Choco-Raspberry Ice Box Cake

An old favorite with a new twist—chill it awhile to let the flavors mellow and make slicing neat

> Preparation time: 15 minutes:
> Chilling time: Several hours.
> Makes 8 servings.

½ cup raspberry preserves
2 tablespoons orange-flavored liqueur
2 packages (two ounces each) whipped topping mix
1 cup cold milk
2 teaspoons vanilla
1 package (8½ ounces) chocolate wafers

1 Combine raspberry preserves and orange flavor liqueur in a cup. Prepare whipped topping mix with milk and vanilla, following label directions.

2 Spread raspberry mixture on one side of a chocolate wafer and whipped topping on second side. Make 10 cooky stacks of coated cookies until all cookies are coated.

3 Turn the first cooky stack on its side on serving tray; spread last cooky with whipped topping and press on the next stack. Repeat until all cookies are joined in a long roll.

4 Frost cake generously with whipped topping. Fit a pastry bag with a fancy tip. Fill bag with remaining whipped topping. Pipe a double row of swirls down the center of cake. Pipe remaining whipped topping around sides and bottom of cake. Spoon remaining raspberry preserves down the top of cake.

5 Chill at least 3 hours. To serve: Cut cake into thin diagonal slices.

Mousse au Chocolat

A smooth, velvety quickie using your electric blender for a time-saver

> Preparation time: 10 minutes.
> Chilling time: 1 hour.
> Makes 8 servings.

1 package (8 ounces) semisweet chocolate pieces
⅓ cup hot, brewed coffee
4 egg yolks

2 tablespoons apricot brandy, or any fruit-
flavored brandy
4 egg whites
3 tablespoons sugar

1 Combine chocolate pieces and hot coffee in
the container of an electric blender; cover container. Whirl at high speed for 30 seconds, or
until smooth.
2 Add egg yolks and brandy to container; cover.
Whirl at high speed 30 seconds.
3 Beat egg whites until foamy and double in
volume in a medium-size bowl; gradually beat
in sugar until well-blended. Fold in chocolate
mixture until no streaks of white remain. Spoon
into 8 parfait glasses or a serving bowl.
4 Chill at least 1 hour. To serve: Garnish with
whipped cream and party candy-patties (from
an 11-ounce package).

Quick Cherry Strudel

Time of preparation is cut to a minimum for this
elegant strudel, when convenient, frozen puff
pastry and prepared pie filling are used

Preparation time: 30 minutes.
Baking time: 25 minutes.
Makes 1 large strudel.

1 package (10 ounces) frozen ready-to-bake
puff pastry shells
1 can (1 pound, 5 ounces) prepared cherry pie
filling
2 teaspoons grated lemon rind
¼ cup packaged bread crumbs
1 tablespoon milk
¼ cup sliced unblanched almonds
2 tablespoons sugar

1 Preheat oven to 450°.
2 Let pastry shells soften at room temperature
for 20 minutes.
3 Combine cherry pie filling and lemon rind in
a small bowl; reserve.
4 On a cloth-lined, well-floured board, overlap
pastry shells in a straight line. Using a floured
stockinette covered rolling pin, press down onto
the pastry shells. (NOTE: You may use a floured
rolling pin without the stockinette, but flour the
rolling pin frequently to prevent the pastry shells
from sticking.) Roll out from center of pastry
shells to a 16x22-inch rectangle, being careful
not to tear pastry.
5 Sprinkle pastry with bread crumbs.
6 Spoon cherry pie filling down length of pastry

closest to you into a 2-inch strip and within 2
inches of edges. Fold in sides; keep filling in.
7 Using the pastry cloth, grasp at both ends
and gently lift the cloth up and let the strudel
roll itself up. Carefully slide onto a cooky sheet,
keeping seam side down, and form into a
horseshoe shape.
8 Brush top generously with milk; sprinkle on
almond slices, pressing well in order to keep
in place. Then sprinkle with sugar.
9 Lower oven heat to hot (400°). Bake 10 minutes or until golden brown; let cool on baking
sheet 10 minutes. Serve the strudel warm.

Baked Alaska

You can make this company spectacular hours
before the big event, then brown it and serve
it at the last minute

Preparation time: 20 minutes.
Freezing time: Several hours.
Bake at 475° for 5 minutes.
Makes 8 servings.

1 pint coffee ice cream
1 pint raspberry sherbet
1 package (2 layers to a package) sponge cake
1 package fluffy frosting mix
Boiling water
Strawberry topping (from a 12-ounce jar)

1 Pack coffee ice cream around the side of a
4-cup bowl (about 6 inches in diameter). Fill
the center with raspberry sherbet; cover bowl
with transparent wrap or aluminum foil. Freeze
a few hours, or until firm.
2 Unmold ice cream by dipping bowl quickly
in and out of a pan of hot water. Turn onto
one sponge layer and return to freezer on a
cooky sheet while preparing frosting.
3 Prepare fluffy frosting mix with hot water,
following label directions. Spread frosting generously over ice cream and sponge layer, being
careful to cover all of the ice cream.
4 Return to freezer until serving time. (May be
made in advance.)
5 Bake in very hot oven (475°) 5 minutes, or
until meringue is golden. Cut into wedges and
serve with strawberry topping.

Shown in the **Top row,** from the left, are: Gâteau de Poires Helene, Easy Cheese Fruit Tarts and Black-bottom Rum Pie. **Middle row:** Peach Melba Bavarian, Coffee Parfait Pie and Mousse au Chocolat. **Bottom row:** Quick Cherry Strudel and Choco-Raspberry Ice Box Cake.

Mocha-Frosted Chocolate Cake

Easy to make with biscuit mix, and it will disappear just as fast

Preparation time: 15 minutes.
Baking time: 30 minutes.
Makes one 9-inch square cake.

1½ cups biscuit mix
¼ cup unsweetened cocoa
¾ cup sugar
2 eggs
⅔ cup milk
3 tablespoons butter or margarine, softened
1½ teaspoons vanilla
1 teaspoon instant coffee powder
1 can (16½ ounces) vanilla frosting

1 Combine biscuit mix, cocoa, sugar, eggs, milk, butter or margarine and vanilla in large bowl. Beat on low speed with electric mixer ½ minute to blend ingredients. Increase the speed to medium and beat for 4 minutes. Scrape the bowl often with a rubber spatula.
2 Turn batter into a buttered 9x9x2-inch baking pan.
3 Bake in moderate oven (350°) 30 minutes, or until center of cake springs back when lightly pressed with finger. Cool cake in pan on wire rack.
4 Combine instant-coffee powder with 2 teaspoons warm water in a small bowl. Stir in vanilla frosting. Swirl frosting on top of cake. Garnish with shaved semi-sweet chocolate, if you wish. Cut cake in squares. Remaining cake may be covered and stored in the pan.

Lemon-Filled Ginger Cake

Here's a winner—spicy cake with a tangy lemon filling

Preparation time: 15 minutes.
Baking time: 30 minutes.
Makes one 9-inch square cake.

1 egg
¾ cup light molasses
⅓ cup butter or margarine, softened
2 cups sifted all-purpose flour
1 teaspoon baking soda
¼ teaspoon salt
1 teaspoon ground ginger
¾ cup milk
1 can (1 pound, 6 ounces) lemon pie filling
10X (confectioners') sugar

1 Combine egg, molasses and butter or margarine in large bowl. Beat with electric mixer until well-blended.
2 Sift flour, baking soda, salt and ginger onto wax paper. Lower mixer speed to very low; add dry ingredients alternately with milk. Mix just until blended. Turn batter into a buttered 9x9x2-inch baking pan.
3 Bake in moderate oven (350°) 30 minutes, or until center of cake springs back when pressed with finger. Cool cake in pan on wire rack about 5 minutes. Turn cake out onto wire rack; cool completely.
4 Split cake into 2 thin layers. Spread bottom layer with lemon filling. Place top layer over filling. Dust top with 10X sugar. Cut into three-inch squares.

Oatmeal-Walnut Cake

Cut into squares and store for special treats

Preparation time: 20 minutes.
Baking time: 45 minutes.
Makes one 9-inch cake.

1 cup boiling water
1 cup quick-cooking oats
2 eggs
2 cups firmly packed brown sugar
¼ cup (½ stick) butter or margarine, softened
1 teaspoon grated lemon rind
1 cup sifted all-purpose flour
1 teaspoon baking soda
1 teaspoon ground cinnamon
1 cup chopped walnuts

1 Pour boiling water over oats; let stand 20 minutes. Water will be absorbed.
2 Combine eggs and brown sugar in large bowl. Beat with electric mixer at medium-high speed until well-blended. Beat in butter and lemon rind.
3 Sift flour, baking soda and cinnamon onto wax paper. Add to egg—brown sugar mixture with oatmeal; mix well. Stir in walnuts. Turn batter into buttered 9x9x2-inch baking pan.
4 Bake in moderate oven (350°) 45 minutes, or until center of cake springs back when lightly pressed with finger. Cool in pan on wire rack. Dust top of cake with 10X sugar, if you wish. Cut into squares. Remaining cake may be covered and stored in the pan.

Index

For your ease in finding a recipe, this index has been divided into two parts: In Cooking in Minutes are fast-cooking dishes, made from scratch. In the second part are dishes which are fast because they use convenience foods.

I COOKING IN MINUTES

See also listings under Pantry Shelf Cooking.

Appetizers:
Artichoke and Mushroom Pot Pie, Tuna, 20
Asparagus Salad, 60
Cheese Log, Pecan, 12
Cheese Mold, Tivoli, 12
Cheese Spread, Appetizer, 11
Crab Spread, Kauai, 10
Frankwiches, Bite Size, 7
Mushrooms, Boursin-Stuffed, 7
Pate Madrilene, 13
Shrimp Salad Silhouettes, 13
Spread, Rosy Hungarian, 13
Tomatoes, Guacamole in Cherry, 8

Desserts:
Apple Betty, 37
Apple Crunch, 37
Apricot-Cake Parfaits, 34
Apricot Creams, 44
Apricot Torte, White Mountain, 41
Banana-Lemon Torte, 46
Butterscotch Chews, 48
Caraway Cubes, 49
Cheese Cake Hawaiian, 43
Chocolate Velvet, 39
Cranberry Cream, 39
Ginger Peachy Shortcake, 34
Grape Parfait, Royal, 43
Grape Snow, Fruity, 34
Lemonade Squares, Pink, 42
Mocha Icebox Roll, 41
Mint Sparkle Sauce, 38
Napolean Creams, 45
Orange Crown Mold, 34
Orange Walnut Cake, 46
Parfait, Frozen Venetian, 43
Peach-Bowl Cheesecake, Party, 41
Peach Cobbler, 35
Peach Melba Sponge, 38
Peach Tortoni, 43
Peanut Drops, 49
Pear Cobbler, Cheddar, 37

Pear Crumble, Stuffed, 38
Pear Praline Cobbler, 38
Pear Whip, Pacific, 33
Praline Crumb Squares, 49
Pumpkin Tarts, 45
Raspberry Mousse Cookie Pie, 45
Raspberry Parfait, Double, 40
Meatballs in Wine Sauce, Castillian, 14
Pepper Steak, Red and Green, 16
Pepperoni and Chick Pea Casserole, 21
Pork Chops Cacciatore, 17
Salmon and Green Bean Puff, Baked, 21
Sausage Pizza, 18
Sausage-Spaghetti Bake, 17
Shrimp Newburg, Jiffy, 19
Sweet-Sour Sauce, 22
Tuna, Artichoke and Mushroom Pot Pie, 20
Veal Parmigiana and Green Noodle Bake, 21
Veal Tonnato, Jiffy, 16

Sandwiches:
Appian Sampler, 24
Baked Puff Sandwiches, 31
Bologna Buns, Hawaiian, 26
Bologna-Cheese Kebash Sandwich, 30
Butter-Crisp Herb Buns, 32
Champ, 30
Cheese Dreams, 29
Cheese for a Crowd, Grilled, 31
Cold-Cut Roll-Ups, 26
Denver Sandwich, 23
Frankfurter Bunwiches, 33
Ham Bounty, 23
Ribbons, 47
Rocky Road Roll-up, 47
Shortcake, February, 36
Ticktacktoe Jewel Cake, 48
Walnut Sticks, 48
Walnut Wafers, 49

Dips:
Anchovy Dip for Raw Vegetables, 8
Bean Onion Dip, 9
Garlic Cheese Dip, 10
Guacamole, 10
Oahu Dip-and-Chip Tray, 8
Spanish Tuna Dip, 10
Sweet-Sour Dip, 9
Tomato Dip, 8

Main Dishes:
Beef and Eggplant Casseroles, 14
Beefburgers, Incredible, 16
Chicken, Barbecued, 14
Chicken Wings, Polynesian, 22
Clam Casserole, 18
Chili Beans and Sausage, 15
Egg Scramble, Marinara, 19
Ham Rolls with Curried Rice, 17
Lamb Chops with Mint and Raisin Pilaf, Orange Glazed, 19
Hot Steak Bunwiches, 33
Meat Loaf Lineup, 32
Melty Mix-Ups, 31
Mediterranean Medley, 23
Milwaukee Stack-Ups, 30

Salmon Jumbos, Simple, 29
Super Subs, 27
Supper Sandwich, 28
Twin Dagwoods on a Skewer, 28
Vienna Heroes, 27

Menus:
Asparagus Salad, 60
Bacon-Cheese Crescents, 52
Beef Platter, Oriental, 57
Berry Bowl, Instant Zabaglione, 54
Cabbage Medley, Sweet-Sour, 50
Cantaloupe Compotes, Frosty, 53
Cheese Relish, Farmhouse, 50
Cheese Salad Plates, Double, 56
Chicken with Rice, Chinese, 58
Coleslaw, Taiwan, 53
Corn Sticks, Snappy, 53
Cucumbers Cairo, 51
Fruit Compote, Spiced, 57
Fruit Cup, Mandarin, 58
Fruits, Appetizer, 55
Halibut Steak, Butter Broiled, 59
Ham and Sweet Potatoes, Deep South, 56
Lemonade Cream, Pink, 52
Meat Ball Hotpot, 51
Nectarine Shortcakes, 51
Noodles, Poppy Seed, 61
Onion Soup, French, 59
Peas in Potato Nests, 62
Peas, Sesame Snow, 59
Pineapple Crescents, Frosted, 60
Pudding Cups, Lemon, 56
Raspberry Cream Stacks, 62
Rice Crown, Ruby
Salad Toss, Continental, 61
Shrimp Appetizer-Salad, 62
Steaks, Quick Saubraten, 50
Squash, Speedy Skillet, 54
Tomatoes, Snowcaps, 60
Veal Goulash, Quick, 61
Veal Napoli, 62
Veal Piccata, 54
Vegetable Rings, Green and Gold, 56

II PANTRY SHELF COOKING:

See also listings under Cooking In Minutes.

Main Dishes:
Beef Stroganoff, Cubed, 72
Beefeater's Platter, 71
Chicken Casserole, Country, 77
Chicken, Colonial, 75
Chicken, Oven Crisp, 77
Chicken, Party, 77
Deep Sea Bake, 80
Fish-and-Shells Italiano, 81
Hash, Red-Flannel, 71
Lasagna, Presto, 82
Macaroni-Tuna Subs, 82
Onion-Sausage Pie, 72

Main Dishes *(continued)*
  Paella, Skillet, 81
  Pizza, 70's, 78
  Salmon Salad Tort, 78
  Sausage Pizza, 75
  Shrimps, Mandarin, 81
  Shrimp and Noodles au Gratin, 82
  Smorgasbord Tuna Salad, 78
  Spaghetti with Clam Sauce, 82
  Steak Piquant, 71
  Stuffed Pancakes Newburg, 80
  Tuna Divan, 79
  Tuna Potpie, 79
  Tuna Roly-Poly, 80
  Tuna with Mushroom Sauce, 78
  Veal, Hungarian, 75
  Veal, Viennese, 72

Salads:

  Baked Alaska, 91
  Bean and Chestnut Bowl, Marinated, 85
  Bean Bowl, Hungarian, 83
  Buffet Mold, 86
  Cheese Fruit Tarts, Easy, 89
  Cherry Strudel, Quick, 91
  Chicken Pasta Picnic Bowl, 88
  Chocolate Cake, Mocha-Frosted, 94
  Chocolate-Raspberry Ice Box Cake, 90
  Crab Salad, 83
  Gateau de Poires Helene, 88
  Ginger Cake, Lemon-Filled, 94
  Grapefruit-Cucumber Toss, 85
  Grapefruit-Aspic Mold, 87
  Ham Mousse in Aspic, 87
  Hero Salad, 88
  Lima Salad Cups, 86
  Oatmeal-Walnut Cake, 94
  Peach Melba Bavarian, 89
  Potato Salad, German, 83
  Rum Pie, Black-Bottom, 89
  Salmon Salad Bowl, Western, 83
  Spinach Salad Imperial, 86
  Yankee Doodle Salad, 84

Soups:

  Clam Stew, 65
  Confetti Chowder, 66
  Country Chicken Chowder, 65
  Finnish Fruit "Soup," 66
  Frosty Tomato Cream, 66
  Mushroom Bisque, 65
  Pea Soup Chowder, 65
  Pea Soup Chowder, 65

Vegetables, 67

  Green Bean Medley, 68
  Onions Mornay, 68
  Potato Medley, Skillet, 70
  Potato Mold, Milano, 70
  Potato Puff, Parisian, 70
  Potatoes Delmonico, 70
  Rice Verde, 68
  Succotash, Creole, 68
  Vegetable, Casserole Creamed, 67
  Vegetables, Duchess, 67
  Vegetables, Savoy Oven, 11